Religion, Society and God

Jim Jones(?) – on politics –

113, 114, 116 117 ('In Conclusion', on influence on democratic freedoms, 121ff etc) · 123. Christian influence on our society, p124 – parish, + establishment, validated. p127 – listening to the people is listening to 'the one from above'

David Jasper – on art, poetry + contemplation + worship. p66, 67 68-9 – disappearance of 'profound religious humanism' = voice of Ch. if not in literature. p71. [illegible] + [illegible] look up 'literature + theology' journal. p74 [illegible]

p107 – Christian teaching – the dignity + worth of each person. p154 religious need/instincts still persist, even with the [illegible] of 'religious organisations' (+ 'big structures') (cf art + poetry?)

p155-156 – mission / evangelism (vision)

p82 freedom/equality – rooted in Christian culture? Can they survive without it?

Religion, Society and God

Public Theology in Action

Edited by
Richard Noake
and
Nicholas Buxton

scm press

Published in 2013 by SCM Press
Editorial office
3rd Floor
Invicta House
108–114 Golden Lane
London EC1Y 0TG

SCM Press is an imprint of Hymns Ancient & Modern Ltd
(a registered charity)
13A Hellesdon Park Road
Norwich NR6 5DR, UK

www.scmpress.co.uk

British Library Cataloguing in Publication data
A catalogue record for this book is available
from the British Library

978-0-334-04926-5

Typeset by Regent Typesetting
Printed and bound by
CPI Group (UK) Ltd

Contents

In fond memory of
Keith Michael Jukes
Dean of Ripon Cathedral, 2007–13
Priest, Pastor and Friend

About the Contributors

Tony Bayfield CBE is a Rabbi and President of the Movement for Reform Judaism in Britain and Lecturer in Personal Theology at Leo Baeck College, London. His DD is from Lambeth, awarded by the Archbishop of Canterbury under his substantive degree-giving powers, for the body of published writing in the field of Christian–Jewish relations.

Nicholas Buxton is Priest in Charge of St John the Baptist Church, Newcastle, and Diocesan Church and Society Advisor for the Diocese of Newcastle. He is the author of *Tantalus and the Pelican: Exploring Monastic Spirituality Today* (Continuum, 2009) and a Visiting Research Fellow at York St John University.

Dan Cohn-Sherbok is an American Rabbi and Professor Emeritus of Judaism at the University of Wales. He is Honorary Professor at Aberystwyth University and Visiting Professor at York St John University.

Daphne Hampson is Professor Emerita of Divinity at the University of St Andrews (chair in Post Christian Thought), and an Associate of the Department of Theology and Religion at Oxford University. She holds doctorates in modern history from Oxford, in theology from Harvard, and a master's in continental philosophy from Warwick. Her most recent book is *Kierkegaard: Exposition and Critique* (Oxford University Press, 2013).

Richard Harries is a life peer, conferred as Baron Harries of Pentregarth in 2006. He was Bishop of Oxford from 1987 to 2006. He is an Emeritus Gresham Professor, and an Honorary Professor of Theology at King's College London. He has written 26 books on the Interface of Christian faith and wider culture, including politics, ethics and the arts. These include *Faith in Politics: Rediscovering the Christian Roots of our Political Values* (Darton, Longman and Todd, 2010) and *The Image of Christ in Modern Art* (Ashgate, 2013).

David Jasper is Professor of Literature and Theology at the University of Glasgow, and Distinguished Overseas Professor at Renmin University of China, Beijing. He holds degrees from Cambridge, Oxford, Durham and Uppsala. He was the first editor of the journal *Literature and Theology*, and his most recent book is *The Sacred Community* (Baylor University Press, 2012).

James Jones was Bishop of Liverpool in 1998–2013 and was previously Bishop of Hull. A former teacher, he has been deeply involved in issues of justice throughout his career. In 2009 he was appointed by the Home Secretary to Chair the Hillsborough Independent Panel, a significant role as the Panel findings have had wide-ranging implications for all those involved in the football stadium disaster.

Estelle Morris is a former MP, for Yardley in Birmingham, and Secretary of State for Education and Skills. In 2005 she was made a life peer and was appointed Pro Vice Chancellor of Sunderland University, a post she held until 2008. She is currently chair of the Executive Group at the Institute of Effective Education at the University of York and is involved in a number of voluntary organizations in both education and the arts.

Richard Noake is Head of the Department of Theology and Religious Studies and Director of the Centre for Church School Education at York St John University. His teaching and research spans religious studies, in particular the diaspora experiences of

Sikhs in the UK; theology, with specific reference to film, popular culture, art and creativity; and education, especially learning and teaching in Higher Education and in Church School contexts. His most recent publication is the co-edited book *Building Communities of Reconciliation Volume II: Christian Responses to Situations of Conflict* (Nanumsa, 2012).

Catherine Pepinster has been editor of *The Tablet* since 2004. She also contributes regularly to 'Thought for the Day' on BBC Radio 4's Today programme, and to national newspapers. She was educated at Manchester University, City University, London, and Heythrop College, University of London, where she completed an MA in Philosophy and Religion.

Mona Siddiqui OBE, is the first Muslim chair in Islamic and Inter-religious Studies in the Divinity School, Edinburgh University. Prior to this she was Professor of Islamic Studies at Glasgow University, where she directed the Centre for the Study of Islam. Her research areas are in Islamic jurisprudence and Christian–Muslim relations. Among her publications are *Christians, Muslims and Jesus* (Yale University Press, 2013), *The Good Muslim: Reflections on Classical Islamic Law and Theology* (Cambridge University Press, 2012), and *The Routledge Reader in Christian–Muslim Relations*, (Routledge, 2012). She also holds visiting professorships at the universities of Utrecht and Tilburg and is an associate scholar at Georgetown University's Berkley Center for Religion, Peace and World Affairs.

Roger Trigg is Senior Research Fellow and Academic Director of the Centre for the Study of Religion in Public Life at Oxford University. He is also Emeritus Professor at Warwick University and author of numerous books and articles focusing on philosophy, social science and the role of religion in public life. His most recent book is *Equality, Freedom and Religion* (Oxford University Press, 2012).

Acknowledgements

The St Wilfrid Lectures were conceived as a response to the growing need for theology to interact with public issues of contemporary society. They began in 2009 as part of the year-long commemorations of the 1300th anniversary of the death of St Wilfrid, Bishop and founder of Ripon Cathedral. This edited collection draws from lectures given in the first three series which tackled the themes of *Rethinking Mission: The Role of the Church in Contemporary Society* (2009), *Religion and Politics: The Role of Faith in Contemporary Society* (2010) and *The Question of God* (2011). Each series provided an opportunity for the general public to engage with six speakers from diverse backgrounds including politics, media, the Church, education and academia. No presumption was made by the members of the St Wilfrid committee as to the personal faith or beliefs of any speaker; however, the context within which these lectures took place was that of 'faith in dialogue with contemporary society', and the intention of the organizers was to provoke debate that relates faith to public concerns and to promote serious reflection on contemporary issues by those of faith and no faith. The lectures are being published in book form to make them available to a wider audience.

The on-going series of lectures is organized by representatives of a four-way ecumenical partnership between Ripon Cathedral (Very Revd Keith Jukes, Revd Dr Nicholas Buxton, Louise Watson, Judith Bustard), York St John University (Richard Noake, Chair, St Wilfrid committee), Methodist District of York and Hull (Revd Graham Carter) and the Diocese of Ripon and Leeds (Revd Canon John Carter, Revd Canon Adrian Alker). The editors and members of the St Wilfrid committee wish to acknowledge those who have made a significant contribution to the St Wilfrid Lecture series since its inception: Eileen Bellett (Cathedral Education Adviser); Andrew Aspland (Head Verger, Ripon Cathedral); the chapter and staff of Ripon Cathedral, including Ken and Sandra Lancaster, Carol Wadey and Loretta Williams; Kathryn Eldred (Senior Administrator), Julian Stern (Dean), Pauline Kollontai (Deputy Dean) and staff of the Faculty of Education and Theology (York St John University); Professor David Fleming, Professor David Maughan-Brown and Professor Sebastian Kim (York St John University); Revd Stephen Burgess (Chair, Methodist District of York and Hull). For the publication of the series, we wish to express our appreciation to Natalie Watson and Mary Matthews at SCM Press, and copy editor Valerie Bingham. We also acknowledge specifically the work of Dr Vicky Nesfield (York St John University) for her sterling efforts in initial editing.

In the final stages of editing the book, the originator of the lecture series and fellow committee member, Keith Jukes, Dean of Ripon Cathedral, tragically and unexpectedly died. He had the vision for the project and never lost sight of the inherent need for the Church and Christian Theology to be in dialogue with the world and the issues that challenge us most. He was always generous of spirit and hospitality, wanting to make all welcome, whatever their religious and political convictions or background. He will be deeply missed as a significant priest, pastor and friend. This book is dedicated to his memory and his contribution.

Introduction

Public Theology in Action

RICHARD NOAKE

The chapters in this edited collection are derived from an on-going lecture series in which academia and Church have provided an opportunity for issues of public concern to be debated in open and public forum. While acknowledging that not all contributors are from a Christian theological, church or even faith perspective, and deliberately so, the fact that the creative vision for and organization of these opportunities has consciously arisen from within an academic and professional context that is avowedly theological sufficiently locates these writings as contributions to Public Theology.

The thread that weaves its way through these ten chapters, as the title foregrounds, is broadly the (continuing) role of faith in contemporary Britain. The specific concerns of this book deal with two areas of significant debate: the question of God in the face of contemporary discourse; and the contribution that religion and those of faith might still make in modern Western society. The discussion about God, from a variety of faith perspectives, highlights diverse concerns relating to new atheism (Richard Harries), genocide (Dan Cohn-Sherbok) and the nature of God's love as expressed in Islam (Mona Siddiqui). This debate about God permeates other chapters, and we are specifically challenged to think how new and different ways of articulating God and being religious might be possible, free of gender bias and inequality (Daphne Hampson). In terms of the contribution of religion to society, we are introduced to a number of important discussions referencing: the arts (David Jasper); freedom and equality (Roger

Trigg); the economy and social teaching (Catherine Pepinster); politics (James Jones); education and schooling (Estelle Morris); and the place of religion in the public square (Tony Bayfield). I argue that these discussions are all prime examples of Public Theology. But for those unfamiliar with this term, what does it mean, and why might it provide a forum for continuing theological engagement?

In *Theology in the Public Sphere: Public Theology as a Catalyst for Open Debate* (2011), Sebastian Kim provides a critical exploration of the task of the Church and theology in not only speaking into, but also being actively engaged in, the public sphere. In the detailed analysis he provides of the particularities of what he and others have termed Public Theology he argues that 'the key word for public theology is public *conversation*, contributing to the formation of personal decisions and collective policy-making in economic, political, religious and social realms' (Kim, p. 3). Kim suggests that there is not one particular method for doing Public Theology, and much of his book is taken up with exploring real ways in which this act of *doing theology publically* is being pursued in different global contexts. However, he does provide a clear, five-point rationale for why it is essential that the Christian Church and theology engages in this way.

First, Kim suggests that the very nature of theology is that it is, or should be, public, and that 'the enquiry and findings are applicable to a wider audience beyond the Christian community because of the evaluative and critical nature of theology and also because its context is not confined to the Church but relates to the kingdom of God' (p. 9). Second, he addresses those who might argue that the bias in theology (and the Christian Church) precludes it from legitimately contributing to conversations about things of public concern because it is not, what he terms, 'neutral'. While he doesn't unpack the substance of the bias or lack of neutrality, I would argue it necessarily includes the specific world view held by the Church and Christian theology that acknowledges the potential for a spiritual and supernatural dimension to living. For some social commentators, this potentially negates the contribution that theology and the Church can bring to debates of public concern, as it does not 'fit' with their world view, seeing it as rooted within non-rational, non-scientific, uncritical, pre-Enlightenment thinking . However, Kim suggests that 'the fact that theology is not "neutral" does not disqualify it from participation in public discussion; on the contrary, because of its distinctive perspective, theological findings can make an effective contribution to public issues' (p. 10).

Kim's third rationale clarifies that 'public' should not be misunderstood as being in contrast to 'personal' or 'private concern', but that 'public' should refer to 'the openness of theology for any party to engage in debate: it is to do with universal access and open debate for all members of the society'(p. 10). His fourth point emphasizes that being 'public' should be viewed as a 'healthy development' for theology, and in this exercise it falls to theologians to 'convince the Christian community of the public relevance of theology and, at the same time, persuade the general public of the necessity of utilizing theological insights in public discussion' (p. 10). His final rationale for Public Theology is the need for 'authenticity' and 'sustainability' – being in the public sphere provokes a requirement for theology to be 'suited to the issues and relevant to the context' (p. 10).

With such considerations before us, it is possible to view these essays as exercises in Public Theology. They meet the essence of Kim's criteria: they were public in the fact that the original context for the essays was a public lecture series, which was provided for and gave open access to the general public; and in publishing them they re-enter the public sphere in a different context and format. They were non-partisan, in terms of audience and contributors: speakers were from different gender and diverse cultural, ethnic and faith or no faith contexts. They addressed issues that resonated with common concerns of the day; their views respectfully listened to, but often at odds with individuals and groups within the audience and certainly with Christian theological perspectives. Selecting speakers from contrasting and potentially (hopefully) challenging contexts was purposeful: it resonates with Kim's concern for Public Theology to afford universal access and open debate, that is that every voice should be listened to and everyone should have opportunity to speak. The audiences were similarly diverse in age, gender and faith or no faith stance; on occasion they were culturally and ethnically diverse too. While acknowledging that the underlying context for the lectures was theological and hence not neutral, nevertheless the intention was very much for intellectual confrontation and contestation to be in evidence. The intention was to challenge not only the audience but also to challenge the Church and theology; Public Theology is not meant to be comfortable, armchair theology. If it is to make a valid contribution to public debate and policy making, Public Theology needs to be challenged and challenging, sustaining and authentic.

We begin the task of publically debating issues that confront church and Christian theology with the thoughts of Richard Harries, who starts by suggesting that we need to take 'serious atheism' seriously. While his essay does not intend to provide a critique of the arguments of serious atheists, what he does do is to suggest that the well-publicized arguments of some new atheists, such as Dawkins, are arguments against beliefs in the kind of God and religion unlikely to be held, recognized or followed by 'most members of the Church of England'. What Harries reflects on and wants to take seriously, in terms of serious atheism, is the challenge that it poses to those of belief to contemplate life without a notion of the divine and what this could bring to our understanding of living. In suspecting this might test those of belief, Harries goes on to argue, through a wealth of references to authors, journalists and artists such as H. L. Mencken, Edward Munch, Samuel Beckett, T. S. Eliot, Emily Dickinson, W. H. Auden and Seamus Heaney, who in their own lives and works have engaged with uncertainty, doubt, scepticism and horror, that this is (or should be) as much a part of the experience of believers as non-believers. Harries would appear to argue that being in relationship with God in this way is more authentic than being caught in uncritical, 'fundamental' belief. He refers to the dangers of talking glibly about the mystery of God and how '(w)e bandy the word G-O-D about as though it was just another card in a card game'. He considers the work of Emily Dickinson who he claims 'knew that the deepest truths had to be hinted at and suggested, told obliquely', and in discussing T. S. Eliot he refers to Eliot's life after conversion as 'co-exist(ing), according to his own account, with a radical scepticism'. Early in his chapter, Harries suggests that most people living in the West, being of the baby-boomer and later generations, have not had to deal with significantly destructive periods in history. Life is, for most, 'easy' and as a result they are not provoked perhaps to ask the big questions. Serious atheism has the power to shake us out of that as it challenges the foundational, albeit latent for most, tendencies in Western culture for (uncritical?) belief. In concluding his chapter, he returns not to the theme of 'serious atheism' but to the poets Seamus Heaney and T. S. Eliot. In Heaney, he finds a poet who spoke little about the metaphysical until later in life, but who has recently commented on transcendence as a 'tendency', and Harries likes the notion that in our relationship with the transcendent, and in dealing with the questions contemplating the divine brings, we need to be encouraged to see faith as being 'on the move, a journey'. In Eliot, the poet of *The Waste Land*, he sees a convert who left none of the possibility of horror behind after conversion but held this alongside a belief in 'a divine purpose that will finally prevail'.

Harries' discussion of God in the face of serious atheism provides a platform on which to consider the question of God through another set of challenging debates, God in the face of the Holocaust. Dan Cohn-Sherbok, in setting the title of his chapter as 'How Odd of God to Choose the Jews' is not leading us essentially to a discussion about chosen-ness, but to a contemplation of God in light of the Holocaust and how a chosen people should now think and believe. In a few short paragraphs Cohn-Sherbok reminds us again of some of the horrors of the Holocaust. He then asks, as many have, 'Where was God when six million died?' His reflections take in the thoughts and writing of significant Jewish contributors to what is termed Holocaust Theology, like Richard Rubenstein and the writer Elie Wiesel. He comments that some, like Rubenstein, argue that after the Holocaust it is no longer possible to believe in a God who acts in history. He references his own work, where he critiqued these Holocaust theologians, and in that critique suggested that what they lacked was an appeal to the 'Hereafter ... the basis of the belief in eternal salvation' that could put the events into a wider context of 'a future life'. However, he now sees shortcomings in his own work and suggests in his new thesis that '(r)ather than develop a modern eschatological Jewish theology based on the experiences of the Jewish people over the centuries ... the time has come for a radical revision of Jewish theology'. What Cohn-Sherbok suggests in this essay, drawing on the work of others who are similarly engaged in this task (David Blumenthal, Arthur Cohen, Melissa Rapheal, Harold Schulweis, Steven Jacobs) is that we need 'a new theological framework consonant with a contemporary understanding of Divine Reality'. His argument, taking in discussion of: Jewish doctrine, Jewish monotheism, the unique place of Jews as receivers of God's revelation, Jewish belief in chosen-ness and God's plan for them, Jewish understanding of Messiah, and ideas of the afterlife, leads him to consider a number of possibilities. First, Judaism has to be seen as one of many potential revelations of God, second, that the notion of being uniquely chosen is difficult to determine and, third, that God cannot be understood any more or less through the events of the Holocaust but needs to be considered as an 'unfathomable mystery'.

Mona Siddiqui provides the third perspective on God from within the Abrahamic tradition in her consideration of Islam and a loving God. It is almost ubiquitous to state that the media portrayal of Islam is universally negative – it is not necessarily the case; what it is easier to state is that the media is unlikely to focus on Islam's portrayal of God as a God of love as it is not the overriding view put forward by Islam. Siddiqui therefore takes on a challenging debate when she considers this premise. She argues that in Islam, God's love is not manifest in a salvific action in history, as in the role of Jesus in Christianity, but is reflected in the different forms of divine communication from God to humanity. Through these prophetic revelations, and for a Muslim through the ultimate revelation given to Muhammad, God's love is revealed. She argues that within Islam there is an inner story of God which has been lost to some extent in what she terms 'the modern preoccupation with prescriptive obedience'. Her considerations take account of various ways in which

Qur'anic and Hadithical literature describe and reflect on God's love, stating that in Islam, while there is no talk of sacrificial or redemptive love, there is nevertheless a clear sense that God is not distant, that he 'knows the secrets of our hearts and is nearer to us than our jugular vein' and that he forgives and shows mercy to all who seek him. It is not surprising that Siddiqui includes in her consideration of God's love the work of Sufi poets, for it is here that the contribution of Islam to the discussion of God's love is perhaps most profound. As she describes and exemplifies, it is in Sufi poetry that 'love for God is all consuming' and where 'love is the central theme of our existence in which human and divine love are inextricably intertwined'.

These first three chapters reflect on ways in which each of the Abrahamic traditions are themselves challenged in their consideration of God. This provides an interesting opportunity for us to reflect on the sophisticated ways in which religions themselves view and discuss the God debate. Daphne Hampson's contribution to this approaches the discussion from a different perspective. Her argument is that we now know (after the Enlightenment) there could not be the historical 'particularity' that the Abrahamic religions, each in their own way, claim. (There could not be one chosen people, or a single human being possessed of a divine nature, or a book that is to be differentiated from all other literature as 'given'.) She argues that it is on account of this claim that adherents of the Abrahamic religions must look to the past, bringing that past into the present as sacred literature, which affects people not least at a subconscious level. Within her discussion, she focuses in particular on the way in which these religions have expressed God, 'his' relationship with humanity and the relationship between and role of men and women, as expressed by these traditions. Her concern is that the hierarchical relationship of male to female has fostered and legitimized male dominance in the societies which have been permeated by these religions. She argues that we need to overcome paradigms that no longer fit with reality as we know it to be, quite apart from the ethical consequences of belief in particularity. Were there such a thing as an interruptive revelation, it would overturn everything that, epistemologically, we have thought we knew. Whatever is the case must necessarily everywhere and at all times be at least potentially the case. Thus, she argues that we should start in the present with our awareness of God. This does not mean that past religions have not acted as 'vehicles' which have carried human awareness of God. But we need now to express that awareness in other form. Theology will become like every other subject, drawing on the past so far as that is useful and creating anew in so far as we need language that conforms to our present knowledge and is gender-inclusive.

The narrative now switches, at least in an explicit sense, from God to a consideration of the role and impact of religion and faith within society. David Jasper, with a particular reflection on art and religion, argues that art and poetry are our 'first guides' in the human quest to fathom 'that which is ever beyond our comprehension'. His discussion encompasses a personal reflection on his own journey to the appreciation of the work of artists and poets, theologians and philosophers in the 'recovery of holiness and of the vision of heaven in the ordinary'. He references the work of various poets: John Donne, George Herbert, Wordsworth, W. H. Auden and more contemporary poets such as David Scott; and artists: van Gogh, Botticelli, Rembrandt and Velasquez. Jasper's own 'art' is in pointing poetically, and creatively crafting a story that locates art and religion as dialogic partners. He uses aspects of his early academic career – his formative work on bringing literature and theology into dialogue – and his more recent experiences at Renmin University in China, where he has worked with the artist Ding Fang, as moments of *poiesis* or 'making'. He speaks of art as almost liturgical and prayerful, and in his description of how he worked with Ding Fang, sharing no common language other than art, how he experienced a moment of '"liturgical living", akin to worship but within the everyday'. What can we take from Jasper's considerations? Perhaps a fresh appreciation of what some have expressed for centuries, that in art and poetry we may see something of the 'beyond'; and that in contemporary Britain we need to continue to support the arts for the possibilities that it brings to speak to us about truths, while acknowledging, as Jasper does, that 'It is never art's task to draw attention to itself or to solve

problems in any limited or immediate way, but to remind and to
bring us to that life which we then each interpret in our own way.'
   We are taken further into this consideration of religion in society with the contributions of Trigg, Pepinster, Jones and Morris.
Their reflections focus on specific societal issues and the possible
ways in which religious discourse can speak into these concerns:
equality and religious freedom; economic challenge and the impact
of Catholic Social Teaching; policy making and Christian values;
and education and schooling. Roger Trigg considers the relationship between freedom to practise one's religion and European
legislation on equality. He references a number of well-known
court cases in the UK where the key issues relate to an individual's
right to practise their understanding of their faith versus equality legislation. He asks what rights might be afforded to people
of religion when placed against equality practices that seem to
be in opposition to their own beliefs. In his considerations, he
raises a number of questions about the place of religion in contemporary British society. He argues that freedom of religion has
been reduced to freedom of worship, and the actual ethics of a
religion relegated, by law, to personal choice, which is superseded
by equality legislation. He talks of 'an underlying antagonism
towards religion, and the view that religion is itself a harmful
influence in society stimulating conflict and division'. What he
concludes, having considered a variety of arguments and stances
on religion in society, is that what is needed is 'freedom *for* religion whereby the potential value of religion in our society is
recognized'. His arguments are well constructed and point to the
on-going debate that some from within faith contexts are having
with an increasingly secular agenda for society put forward by, to
coin Harries' phrase, 'serious atheism'.
   Catherine Pepinster focuses on a number of key challenges that
we face in modern society, with the main thrust of her argument
being a consideration of the recent economic crisis and collapse in
the West. For her, the teachings of the Catholic Church, as represented within Catholic Social Teaching, provides an affirming
narrative through which to see the best of human flourishing and
relationships. She argues that in understanding how to be effec-

tive neighbours, underpinned by the ethics of Christian teaching, we can find ways to address the challenges we face. In all this, positive human relationships need to be bounded by notions of: solidarity, that which creates obligation between persons that challenge exploitation and oppression of the other; and of subsidiarity, the need to make and take decisions at the closest point to the people that they will directly affect. She postulates that God is found incarnated in the best of human relations where people are protected and nourished by community but liberated to be creative individuals.

James Jones reflects, broadly speaking, on the impact of Christian values on public life and policy making in his consideration of the place of religion in politics. He references issues as diverse as freedom of speech, freedom of expression, justice and fairness, the role of the family and support for marriage, support for the 'other' and in particular migrant communities, and issues relating to ecology and the future of the planet. All these areas, he considers, resonate with political currency; the Church should be in all of these debates, but he argues that it should be neutral on party politics. He talks throughout of the need to bring spiritual, economic and social renewal and reform together to have lasting impact in areas of social deprivation and he cites a number of key initiatives he has championed and seen develop. He advocates, implicitly, the need for those of faith to be at the heart of the struggle for equality and fairness agendas and to 'ensure greater opportunities especially for disadvantaged children and young people'. He concludes, interestingly, with a note about the role of bishops in the House of Lords and how they need to listen to the people and in doing so may be listening to God.

The fourth chapter to focus on a specific societal concern is Estelle Morris' consideration of education and schooling with specific reference to the role of church schools within compulsory state provision offered in England and Wales. She opens by providing the historical context for schools of a religious foundation within the compulsory schooling system. The Churches provided schools for the 'poor' long before the state stepped in and today they still provide one third of state schools in England. In bringing the history up to the present Morris identifies that we now have a funding system that provides for not only Church of England, Methodist, Roman Catholic and Jewish schools but, following legislation under the last Labour Government, the State now funds a number of Muslim, Sikh and non-conformist groups. From this context, she then highlights what some of the arguments for and against the state funding of what she terms 'faith schools' includes and then asks some pertinent questions about the future for these schools. As she rightly identifies, the continuation of state funding for schools with a religious foundation can be a contentious issue and one that certain vocal lobbies, like the secular humanists, petition against. Those who argue for such schools cite, among other reasons, the academic success often associated with such schools, while opponents say this is to be expected given the likely selection procedures and demographic using the school. Opponents raise the issue of the continual societal segregation these schools promote, particularly in mixed-faith communities. She suggests that even if this is not the case such schools need to examine the roles they play in society and must have at the heart of their approach the need to be 'forces for understanding, for teaching tolerance, for broadening horizons and building bridges'. Morris very much sees the challenge to 'faith schools' being the central purpose of the school. Is it to 'create a school based on a particular set of values or one based on a particular set of religious beliefs'? What she would appear to celebrate is strong teaching on ethical and moral living against the potential for indoctrination into a religious belief system. Her final comment is a pertinent one: '... what contribution will they [faith schools] make to educating a generation of young people who will achieve greater cohesion, understanding and solidarity than the generation who have gone before them'.

The final chapter comes from Tony Bayfield, who carefully brings us back in many ways to the notion of Public Theology, albeit with strong hints of the Jewish to better flavour our discussions. His considerations of the role of religion and the religious to the public square is insightfully stated, taking in something of the history of religions engaging with society, the impact of the

Enlightenment, debates about the public square and the rise of religious and secular fundamentalism. In discussing where those of faith should be seated within the public square, he advocates what Rowan Williams calls procedural secularism which 'seeks to allow all faith perspectives equal access to the public realm but claims to confer no political privilege on any'. What he concludes is that society is not secular, it is plural, and all have to play a part in its future. He argues that those of faith, if they are to be taken seriously, need to use the lingua franca of the day, which is the language of reason, and should be less concerned with playing the 'Jesus is Lord' card. As he states, 'Christianity in the market place may need to speak the language of the market place and rely on the undoubted quality of the spiritual, intellectual and ethical fruits on offer to sell itself.' His final considerations are that those of faith should be given access to the public square and that 'contributing with reason, sensitivity and humility to the public debate … is the very essence of democracy. We people of faith can be faithful democrats just as much as the divines of secularity.'

In tandem with many of the contributors to this book, I would argue that the role of the Church, of theology and more broadly of those of faith is to be in the public square engaged in the debates that are most important to our communities and society. As my colleague Sebastian Kim also says, 'Public Theology is not purely an academic endeavour to be developed in academia and then conveyed to the wider public, but rather this type of theology has to be in interaction with churches, faith communities and wider society and, in turn, inform academia of its findings' (Kim and Draper 2008, p. 144). The lectures that inspired these chapters began life as interactions with the public and now return as reflections and considerations to be shared with an even wider public.

Bibliography

Sebastian C. H. Kim, 2011, *Theology in the Public Sphere: Public Theology as a Catalyst for Open Debate*, London: SCM Press.
Sebastian C. H. Kim and Jonathan Draper, 2008, *Liberating Texts? Sacred Scriptures in Public Life*, London: SPCK.

I

God Outside the Box: On Taking Serious Atheism Seriously

RICHARD HARRIES

One of the features of the current religious scene in the UK is the absence of a serious encounter with atheism. You may find this statement surprising. After all, the attack dogs of the new atheism, Richard Dawkins, Christopher Hitchins and their peers, have had huge publicity over the past ten years and their books sell in the millions. But although a fair number of people have had their anti-religious feelings affirmed by such writers, I suspect that they have failed to make much impression on the minds of either religious believers or more open-minded non-believers. This is because the kind of religion that Richard Dawkins, for example, attacks so strongly is not that shared by most members of the Church of England. His target is fundamentalists who are opposed to evolution. Such people, in their turn, like to suggest that a belief in evolution is integrally linked with hostility to religion. In short, Richard Dawkins and the fundamentalists feed on one another and need one another. The consequence is that most members of the mainstream Churches, and many others who, though without a faith are open-minded, do not feel that such a debate 'speaks to their condition', to use an old phrase.

The Baby-Boom Condition

The Dawkins–fundamentalist debate is often part of a wider one, that between science and religion, which though interesting and important, is not one that is likely to sweep religious believers off their rock of faith into the sea of unbelief. For the fact of the matter is that the vast majority of people, however much they might respect the achievements of science, know that there are certain questions that, however we answer them, cannot be addressed as though they were propositions to be tested out in a laboratory. The result is that the percentage of scientists who are religious believers is much the same as it is for the population as a whole. There are a range of factors which influence people to believe or disbelieve, but the strength of the scientific method, for all its real achievements, is not, for most, the decisive factor.

One unintended consequence of the association of atheism with the atheism of Richard Dawkins is that we do not have a debate about what I judge to be more serious and important forms of atheism. I intend to suggest here that it is fundamental to faith that religious believers do fully face these other forms of atheism. There is an overlooked reason why a more serious atheism is not on the agenda at the moment. This is because in recent decades the world has been dominated by the so-called baby-boomers, those born after the Second World War who came of age in the 1960s. This is a generation who have never had to fight a major war, who have had a standard of living that is unprecedented in human history, who are healthier and who will live longer than any previous generation, many of whom are on final salary pensions, and who can fill their lives with interesting things to do. Harries' sod's law states that for happiness we need three things: health, time and money, but until now nature has contrived to deny us one of the three. When we are young, we have health and time but no money. When we are middle-aged, we have health and money but not time. When we are old, we have time and money but no health. But now for the first time, the law has been broken. The generation that came of age in the 1960s, and probably their children, are living well into their 80s, keeping healthy, have golden pensions and are able to take that third cruise in the year.

I do not of course ignore the personal tragedies, illnesses, broken relationships and early deaths, which will always be part of life. Nor do I ignore the fact that what I have said does not apply to everyone. For example, if you are a man living in parts of Glasgow, your life expectancy will be ten years shorter than if you live in the South East of England, or even other parts of Glasgow, and that gap has significantly widened over the past 20 years. However, when we think of the wider forces that govern life the past 50 years have been quite extraordinary. Linda Grant entitled her most recent novel *We Had It So Good* about the generation I have described, and to which she herself belongs. She has said about herself and her contemporaries that history has not impinged on them in any destructive way, unlike almost every other generation in the past.

One effect of this is that there has been little incentive to raise the big questions in life. Life is busy, full of interesting things to do to fill the time – the next skiing holiday, the next cruise. The media is increasingly dominated by lifestyle articles and programmes on cooking, gardening and travel. All of this is great. I relish the good things of life as much as anyone. But it is such a contrast with the reality of life for the vast majority of people in history and the rest of the world today, where life is a daily struggle simply to exist. Where life is a battle to survive, one tends to be both more open to the big question of what it might all be about, and more in need of the spiritual strength to continue. Where this is not the case, as in the prosperous West, we have been able to skim along on the surface of life, without having to engage at any deep level with the big questions. This, allied to the great ignorance there is now about the Christian faith in our society, and the association in people's mind of religion with extremism, strife and violence, means that the default position for young people growing up is to disbelieve. The knee-jerk reaction to the question whether they believe in God in any orthodox sense for so many is 'No'. Or, they may express hostility to religion while defining themselves in some sense as spiritual. This for many is not a reply that has emerged as a result of any serious thought or struggle, but is simply the default position of a society that has wanted to busy itself with all the many interesting things there are today to do and enjoy.

The subtitle of my book *God Outside the Box* is *Why Spiritual People Object to Christianity* (Harries, 2002). In the book,

I consider the strong feelings of many people who regard themselves as spiritual but who regard the Christian faith they have encountered as morally objectionable in some way; for one of the major changes in the atheism of today compared with most forms in the past, is that it claims the moral high ground. It is not just that Christianity is untrue, it is, according to Hitchins, a poison that needs to be pumped out of the stomach of society. My 21 chapters consider the different kinds of moral objections to Christian faith. What I said there is, I believe, still highly relevant. However, the theme of this chapter here, is *On Taking Serious Atheism Seriously*. I have suggested that so much of what passes for atheism today is not the serious atheism I have in mind. So allow me to start elsewhere, with someone rather surprising, the man generally regarded as one of the most astute and funny observers of the human scene in the twentieth century, the American journalist H. L. Mencken, whose aphorisms are in a class of their own. His writings have recently been published in full, and among them is this statement:

> Once I ventured the guess that men worked in response to a vague inner urge for self-expression ... An hypothesis with rather more plausibility in it now suggests itself. It is that men work simply in order to escape the depressing agony of contemplating life – that their work like their play, is a mumbo-jumbo that serves them by permitting them to escape from reality ... Man cannot sit still, contemplating his destiny in this world without going frantic. So he invents ways to take his mind off the horror. He works. He plays. He accumulates the preposterous nothing called property. He strives for the coy eye-wink of fame. He founds a family and spreads his curse over others. All the while the thing that moves him is simply the yearning to lose himself, to forget himself, to escape the tragic-comedy that is himself. Life, fundamentally, is not worth living. (Mencken, 2010)

I could spend some time analysing and reinforcing the sentiments in that statement, but I will just pick out one word, 'horror'.

Recently in church we prayed for all vulnerable children who were in danger of being abused. I thought of all the children in the world who at that very moment were actually being abused, either sexually or by violence, or often by both, who were being trafficked into prostitution or bonded labour. I thought of them and all that anguish crying out to God. But the thought is unbearable, so it cannot be imaginatively entered into for more than a split second. One of the most iconic paintings of the twentieth century was Edward Munch's *The Scream*, which simply shows a person going over a bridge uttering or about to utter a scream in a way that fills the whole scene. That scream continues. It is most obvious in relation to the kind of anguish just mentioned, but it goes wider than that to refer to the universal human experience of being a limited, finite consciousness locked in a human body, 'half ape, half angel' as Disraeli put it; able with our minds to explore the universe, and with our souls to reach out to what is eternal, yet at the mercy of frail human flesh and all the vicissitudes of nature and history.

It is a theme that could be illustrated in many ways. I will simply state that the writers I most admire are those who experience life in this way and who survive on the basis of humour or faith or a combination of both. It was humour in the case of Mencken, particularly satire, but there are people such as Jonathan Swift, the great Dean of St Patrick's, Dublin, whose memorial refers to his *saeva indignatio* (his savage indignation) or Evelyn Waugh, who combine fierce satire with a serious Christian faith. Two other writers I admire are Dr Johnson and Samuel Beckett. It is no accident that Samuel Beckett started to write a play about Johnson. They both felt that getting through our days was a matter of filling up what they called the vacuity at the heart of life, though Johnson combined this with a passionate Christian faith, while Beckett's stance is less easy to define.

A Literary Response to Religion: Beckett and Eliot

I have been fortunate enough to see some outstanding performances of Beckett's plays, and two in particular haunt my mind
still. These were performances of his play *Happy Days*, first of
all with Peggy Ashcroft in the central role of Winnie, and then
with Billy Whitelaw in the same part. The stage is bare except
for Winnie in the middle in a pile of sand. During the first act,
the sand reaches up to her waist. In the second act, it reaches
her neck, so only her head is showing. A fierce light beats down.
There is one other character, her husband Willie, who lies on the
stage just away from the heap of sand but trying to edge his way
towards it, who is speechless and who has perhaps lost his mind.
There is a revolver there, and we do not know if he is going to
make use of it, but it lies there with its hint of menace. For the
whole of the play, Winnie conducts a monologue. Here is a brief
excerpt towards the beginning, with Winnie taking things out of
her handbag, at this point her spectacles.

> Marvellous gift – (*stops polishing, lays down spectacles*) – wish
> I had it – (*folds handkerchief*) – ah well – (*puts handkerchief
> back in bodice*) – can't complain – (*Looks for spectacles*) –
> no no – (*takes up spectacles*) – mustn't complain – (*holds up
> spectacles, looks through lens*) – so much to be thankful for
> – (*looks through other lens*) – no pain – (puts on spectacles) –
> hardly any – (Beckett, 1966, p. 12)

And so it goes on for the whole evening. I hope that even from the
short excerpt given, the point is clear. The heap of sand getting
ever higher is of course a symbol of our mortality, the revolver
a hint of the aggression that lies just below the surface in so
many relationships. Above all, there is the courageous attempt
by Winnie to keep herself going, to keep her spirits up, with little
sayings, including prayers, and by continually fiddling with things
in her handbag. It is a performance that evokes a sense of horror,
for that is what life can be like, particularly when we are old. Yet
the performance also evokes a sense of pathos, pity and compas-

sion for Winnie's courage in going on, continually trying to buck herself up, in an old-fashioned way.

Beckett's own religious position is difficult to categorize. Though usually thought of as an atheist, he has been described as a secular mystic, and a Christ-haunted man. Whatever it was, behind it was the bleakest realism. Serious atheism, with which I am concerned, faces and feels life as Beckett conveys it. It continues as atheism in so far as it remains impossible to reconcile that sense of horror with belief that there is a wise and loving power behind, beyond and within all things. Beckett has clearly pondered that question long and hard, and conveyed his feelings with wonderful poetry and great humour. An example of this humour is found in his play *Endgame*. A character called Nagg tells a story about a man who asks his tailor to make him a pair of trousers. Some days later the man calls in and finds that the tailor has made a mess of the seat. He is understanding, but when he returns a few days later, he finds that the tailor has got the crotch all wrong. Again he is patient, but when he comes back after ten days, he finds that the flies are a mess, and so it goes on. At last, in exasperation, the man cries out that if God can make the world in six days, then surely a pair of trousers should not take three months. The tailor responds by disdainfully comparing the parlous state of the world with his wonderful trousers! I would like to suggest that the Christian believer, no less than the person who remains an atheist, feels this, both the horror of existence and how it seems incompatible with faith in a wise and benevolent creator. And that raises a question about the nature of faith.

I should emphasize at this stage that this horror, this vacuity, is not all we experience in life. Most of us will on many occasions have been conscious of life as good, as a wonderful blessing. We have known people we admire, people with streaks of genuine goodness and courage. It is the presence of this other wonderful side to life which makes the dilemma so intense. If life were simply horror, we would all commit suicide. But it isn't. And the reason we go on going on is not just the animal will to survive long enough to breed, but because of a half-sensed intuition that something great is at stake. So we live poised between a consciousness of life as a blessed gift and what a Beckett character calls the punishment for having been born. This is the dilemma that gives rise to what is termed the problem of evil. I will not go into this dilemma here, although I do devote a chapter to this crucial issue at the end of *God Outside the Box*.

What I am concerned with now is the bringing together of this serious atheism and the Christian faith. One of the best known converts to the Christian faith in the twentieth century was T. S. Eliot. One of the features of his faith that is unusual and little known is that way he combined it with continuing scepticism and radical doubt. He much admired Pascal, who had a similar outlook. So, for example, Eliot wrote of Pascal that he was

[t]he type of one kind of religious believer, which is highly passionate and ardent, but passionate only through a powerful and regulated intellect ... facing unflinchingly the demon of doubt which is inseparable from the spirit of belief. (Smart, 2010, p. 8)

Eliot was brought up as a Unitarian, but became highly critical of Unitarianism, and of all religions and philosophies that he judged to be vague and indecisive. He himself adopted a religion of clear and definite dogmas, the Anglo-Catholicism of the 1920s, and was a serious observer of this in its most ritualistic form. But though deeply religious, he was the opposite of a zealot and indeed hated zealotry of any kind. This was, I suggest, because he continued to allow his deeply sceptical side to remain part of his consciousness. As he reflected in 1948, 21 years after his conversion:

The more conscious becomes the belief, so the more conscious becomes unbelief: indifference, doubt and scepticism appear ... A higher religion imposes a conflict, a division, torment and struggle within the individual. (Smart, p. 155)

Smart similarly wrote of Eliot, 'the crux of Eliot's Christianity, what made it unusual, interesting and so distant from Unitarianism was that it incorporated so much doubt' (p. 269). If Eliot is correct in his understanding of faith, it means that the adoption of the Christian faith, far from making an end to the sceptical side of our mind, will in fact heighten it. It will heighten it, because it has to live side by side with its challenging, hopeful opposite. Furthermore, for Eliot, it is faith in a clear and definite form which is able to incorporate this scepticism, and it may be that it is just this combination which enables a person to have a faith that is at once clear, firm and committed but without a trace of oppressive zeal.

But how can such scepticism, such radical doubt, live in the same mind and heart as religious faith? Surely, we have been brought up to think that they are the opposites? Faith banishes doubt, and scepticism undermines faith. Faith, after all, is something you stake your life on. It seems to demand absolute certainty. How can it live in the same mind as that which attempts to destroy its very foundation? It is an important question, but before addressing it, I must make my main point, which is that in taking serious atheism seriously, the Christian, as much as the open-minded unbeliever, will be open to the horror of existence as well as the sublime story of divine love that never gives up on us. Or, to put it another way, as the full horror of life dawns on us, so too does the possibility that life's meaning cannot be contained in ordinary categories and tidy schemes. An awareness that there is something else here, something quite extraordinary, unbelievably wonderful, and truly awesome slips into the mind and heart. At the risk of putting forward just another of those neat, tidy schemes, I must try to summarize just what that story is.

Serious Atheism and Challenges to Religious Belief

God has given the universe a real independence, a freedom which comes to consciousness in us. Indeed, if we think about it, this is what must be meant by the idea of creation. To be created is to have a life of one's own, whether it is an electron, a cell or a multi-cell organism such as ourselves. So we find ourselves alive, conscious of life as a miraculous blessing, full of good things, surrounded by people who have the capacity for great kindness and sometimes heroic virtue. At the same time, we are daily aware of the most terrible cruelties and suffering, of what must be called evil. Sometimes they are so terrible that, like Elie Wiesel in relation to the Holocaust, we can only respond: 'How is one to speak of it? How can one not speak of it?' We can only respond with an appalled silence not just in relation to the Holocaust but to many other cruelties, although, as Wiesel also argued, we have to bear witness to the truth however terrible (Wiesel, 1990, pp. 191–202).

The Christian claim is that God himself has entered into the flux of human history and suffered its consequences to the point of an agonized death, and that in doing so he has united heaven and earth, God and humanity in a union that can never be broken. He has entered our hell and even there holds us close to himself in a way that can never be sundered. He did this uniquely in Jesus, but what he does in him, he does through him, for every human being. Uniting humanity in himself, he holds us close to the Father and indwells us with his spirit. This is more than a matter of being with and alongside us, important though that is. For the Divine Life in Christ unites heaven and earth in a way which cannot be destroyed. This is what the apostles discovered on the third day. The life they had known in Jesus was revealed to be eternally one with the Father, and was with them still, raised to a universal contemporaneity. Their lives were now one with his for ever. They were 'in Christ'. Nothing could separate them from the love of God.

In relation to this story, it is necessary to make one obvious point. The ultimate value of life cannot be judged simply by weighing the amount of pleasure against the amount of pain. If you put your life on the scales and balance the pleasure of it against the pain, I hope you will find, as I do, that the pleasure outweighs the pain. But if you take the whole of human history, or much of the world today, can that be said? We don't know, for we have not asked everyone, but it is not obvious that it does. So if there is a good purpose behind life, it cannot be understood simply in terms of a utilitarian calculus of pain and pleasure. Don't get me wrong. I dislike pain as much as most of us, and I enjoy my pleasures. We rightly do what we can to help others out of their pain, and increase their happiness. But if we believe that there is a good purpose to life and a good outcome to it, we must put something other than pain and pleasure on the scales. What this is, quite simply, is our capacity to transcend our native egoism in a genuine desire for the good of others, a desire that is ultimately rooted in God, and that finds its final flourishing in relation to him.

What I have suggested so far then, is that if we allow ourselves to face honestly the bleakness and horror of life from an atheistic perspective, we will at the same time allow ourselves to be open to experience the compelling power of the Christian story. Furthermore, I have quoted Eliot to the effect that a mature faith can and perhaps ought to co-exist with a radical scepticism. Yet how can this be? As I have said, surely faith demands certainty? After all, Saint Paul said that if Christ was not raised, we Christians are the most miserable of all people. He and countless others have literally staked their lives on its truth. Take even the less extreme case of someone offering themselves for ordination. How can they give their whole life over to something that they are not certain about, and which a good number of other people they much respect think is nonsense? So we need to think a little about the relationship between certainty and faith.

Strictly speaking only deductive truths are absolutely certain, that is, those truths which consist of drawing out the conclusions that are already built into the definition. For example: 'All cats have four feet. Kitty is a cat. Kitty has four feet.' That is certain if rather un-illuminating. The so-called ontological argument, which continues to fascinate philosophers, argues that the existence of God is likewise true by definition. However, to put it somewhat technically, existence is not a predicate, and the argument does not work.

Inductive truths can be to all intents and purposes certain. 'The sun will rise tomorrow' is one example. Hypothetically that could be untrue, after all, the universe might come to end, or the laws of gravity could be reversed. But unless the word certain is going to lose all meaning, I think it can be usefully used about this kind of statement. The existence of God cannot be certain in that sense, for it cannot be tested in the way that conforms to scientific method. It is not open to either verification or falsification in this life.

The traditional proofs for the existence of God do not work. In my view, all so-called proofs simply leave the matter open, for reasons I will not digress into here. This does not mean to say that faith is unreasonable. On the contrary, I myself believe that it is religious faith which helps us to account not only for the existence of anything at all, but also for our experience of morality and beauty, the order of the universe, and our capacity for both good and evil. The Christian faith gives a more coherent and consistent account of all this than any other alternative. So faith can be a reasonable faith in that sense. But that does not make it certain. For there is no way we can show logically why the existence of the universe should make sense, or should be understood in reasonable terms. Kant was right. We have no way of showing that the kind of reasoning which applies within the world applies to the questions about why the world is here in the first place. To assume it does is to assume an answer to the question we are asking in the first place. It begs the question.

So it seems that we cannot use the word certainty about faith at all. Yet, the poet Gerard Manley Hopkins could write to his friend and fellow writer Robert Bridges to say, 'You do not mean by mystery what a Catholic does. You mean an interesting uncertainty ... But a Catholic by mystery means an incomprehensible certainty' (Hopkins in Phillips, 1990, p. 194). Religious people very often do feel that God, though incomprehensible, is so much part of their whole understanding of life, their very being, that the reality of what they believe seems certain. This may be a powerful witness; nevertheless it does not always, or even very often, convince the non-believer, who always has another explanation at hand for that faith, and the felt certainty that is claimed for it. Furthermore, we know that some of the most deluded people claim certainty for their wrong-headed beliefs.

I therefore believe that we have to look at what is at the heart of Christianity, at least according to St Paul's great hymn in

1 Corinthians 13: faith, hope and love. It is above all a faith, not simply in believing certain things to be true, but a deep trust and commitment. It is a hope, in that it is in the future that the truth of faith will be vindicated. It is love, in that it is commitment to a way of life now, rooted in faith and sustained by hope. The three are interlinked. For although Paul contrasts sight and hope, 'Now to see something is no longer to hope: why hope for what is already seen?' (Rom. 8.24 RSV), he also says 'Hope does not disappoint us, because God's love has been poured into our hearts through the Holy Spirit that has been given to us' (Rom. 5.5).

I believe that Christianity is committed to the truth of certain propositions. It is not just a matter of the feelings or a way of life. It involves not intellectual assent. But the mind does not act alone, the whole person moves. So assent is integrally linked to a way of seeing life and living it. What matters is not the sceptical alternative, which can arise in the mind at any time, but wholeheartedness and consistency in the way of life. So many ordinary Christians would want to say with the Psalmist 'Taste and see how Good the Lord is' (Ps. 34.8).

What is it that puts so many off the Christian faith today? One factor is the way that religious believers, and I include myself, have a tendency to talk too glibly, too easily about the mystery in whom we live and move and have our being. We bandy the word G-O-D about as though it was just another card in a card game. But that word indicates a reality which by definition makes a total difference to our lives, one difference being a sense of wonder and awe. John of Damascus, who lived in the eighth century, was not only himself impeccably orthodox, but he has also long been taken as a standard of orthodoxy, particularly for the Eastern Church. He wrote, 'It is plain, then, that there is a God. But what he is in his essence and nature is absolutely incomprehensible and unknowable' (John of Damascus, 1983, Vol. IV).

Two poets who really understood what it is that religious truth could not and should not say were Emily Dickinson and W. H. Auden. In 1868, Emily Dickinson wrote:

Tell all the truth but tell it slant –
Success in circuit lies
Too bright for our infirm delight
The truth superb surprise
As lightning to the children of Eve
With explanation kind
The truth must dazzle gradually
Or every man be blind.

(Dickinson in Johnson, 1970, p. 506)

W. H. Auden wrote a poem whose title was a quotation from someone else, The Truest Poetry is the Most Feigning, which accurately sums up its theme. He ends by describing the ambiguous nature of human beings 'Imago Dei who forgot his station', and asks the question:

What but tall tales, the luck of verbal playing,
Can trick his lying nature into saying
That love, or truth in any serious sense,
Like Orthodoxy, is a reticence?

(Auden, 1976, p. 470)

Emily Dickinson knew that the deepest truths had to be hinted at and suggested, told obliquely. W. H. Auden knew that serious truth and true Orthodoxy is also a reticence. Many people who would not describe themselves as religious instinctively feel this. So do many of those who are feeling their way along the path of spiritual truth but who are put off by the clichés and banalities of so much conventional religion.

What it Means to be a Christian

It may be that we now live in a time in which religious words and phrases have been so over used and so cheapened that we are called to silence. Certainly this is what Dietrich Bonhoeffer believed. While in prison for his role in the attempted assassination of Hitler, he wrote Thoughts on the Baptism of D W R:

Today you are being baptised as a Christian. The ancient words of the Christian proclamation will be uttered over you, and the command of Jesus to baptise will be performed over you, without your knowing anything about it. But we too are being driven back to first principles. Atonement and redemption, regeneration, the Holy Ghost, the love of our enemies, the cross and resurrection, life in Christ and Christian discipleship – all these things have become so problematic and so remote that we hardly dare anymore to speak of them … So our traditional language must perforce become powerless and remain silent and our Christianity today will be confined to praying for and doing right by our fellow men … But the day will come when men will be called again to utter the word of God with such power as will change and renew the world … Until then the Christian cause will be a silent and hidden affair, but there will be those who pray and do right and wait for God's own time. (Bonhoeffer, 1962, p. 160)

Recently, I read the transcript of a wonderful conversation between the Nobel Prize-winning poet Seamus Heaney and another wonderful poet, Jon Stallworthy. Most of Heaney's poems have evoked his childhood world on a farm in Northern Ireland, and have not touched much on what we might call metaphysical concerns. Not long ago, he had a serious stroke, but after a while he began to write poetry again, and he started to recall his deeply religious upbringing, what he called his 'childhood radiance world', which, though it was destructively controlling, had 'a sense of glory and eternity'. In the conversation with Jon Stallworthy, after recounting this, he went on to say that although he would not want to give up on transcendence, he was nevertheless wary of it: religious absolutism, he felt, robs us of something. At which point Jon Stallworthy commented that it was 'rather life-denying'. The theme of religion as life-denying was a major one in the literature of the twentieth century. But, according to that conversation, it was the absoluteness of religion linked with its controlling function that made for this. Instead, Heaney posits transcendence as a direction one might tend towards in contrast to the 'Dawkins direction'. I will finally reflect on that image.

The idea of a direction in which you tend implies being on the move, a journey. You are not staying put, where you are. It implies that you have not yet arrived. You cannot describe from first-hand experience the goal of your journey. But you have a direction, and you have some idea of what the consummation may be like. You cannot describe Santiago de Compostella because you have never been there. But you know the direction, the route has been well travelled before you, and you have heard tell of things such as the great bell in the cathedral. But the main thing is that you are on your way. You have set out and you are walking, staff in hand. It is the image of a journey that runs through T. S. Eliot's *Four Quartets*. There he wrote that to 'apprehend the point of intersection of the timeless with time is an occupation for the saint', in a life of 'selflessness and self-surrender'. That same 'prayer, observance, discipline, thought and action' was very much part of Eliot's own life after his conversion to the Christian faith. It co-existed, according to his own account, with a radical scepticism. I think it is no surprise that before his conversion he was above all the poet of *The Waste Land*. He knew the horror of life at first hand and became the voice of the generation of the 1920s and '30s who experienced life in the same bleak way. Becoming a Christian did not, I think, mean that he left behind the possibility of that horror. It intensified it as the alternative to what he had by then committed his life to. This was that, despite so many appearances to the contrary, life expresses the purpose of a wise and loving power, one who has united his undying life with ours, and who calls us to live in him a life of trust, hope and love; and in so doing, to be signs of a divine purpose that will finally prevail.

Bibliography

W. H. Auden, 1976, 'The Truest Poetry is the Most Feigning': *Collected Poems*, London: Faber and Faber.
Samuel Beckett, 1976, *Endgame*, London: Faber and Faber.
Samuel Beckett, 1966, *Happy Days*, London: Faber and Faber.

Dietrich Bonhoeffer, 1962, *Letters and Papers from Prison*, London: SCM Press.

John of Damascus, 'Exposition of the Orthodox Faith', in 1983, *I, 4, Nicene and Post-Nicene Fathers Vol. IV*, Grand Rapids: Eerdmans.

T. S. Eliot, 1969, *Four Quartets: The Complete Poems and Plays of T. S. Eliot*, London: Faber and Faber.

Richard Harries, 2002, *God Outside the Box: Why Spiritual People Object to Christianity*, London: SPCK.

G. M. Hopkins, 'Letter to Robert Bridges, October 24th 1883', in Catherine Phillips, ed., 1990, *Gerard Manley Hopkins: Selected Letters*, Oxford: Clarendon.

Thomas H. Johnson, ed., 1970, *Emily Dickinson: the Complete Poems*, London: Faber and Faber.

H. L. Mencken, Marion Rogers, eds, 2010, *Prejudices, Final Volume*, New York: Library of America.

Barry Smart, 2010, *Anglo-Catholic in Religion: T. S. Eliot and Christianity*, Cambridge: Lutterworth.

Elie Wiesel, 1990, 'When Memory Brings People Together' (Address to the Reichstag, 10 November 1987), in *From the Kingdom of Memory*, New York: Schocken Books, pp. 191–202.

2

How Odd of God to Choose the Jews

DAN COHN-SHERBOK

For thousands of years Jews have asserted that they are God's special people. In the Book of Deuteronomy, the Lord proclaims: 'For you are a people holy to the Lord your God: the Lord; your God has chosen you to be a people for his own possession out of all peoples that are on the face of the earth' (Deut. 7.6 RSV). According to tradition, God watches over the Jewish nation, guiding his people to their ultimate destiny. Divine choice demands reciprocal response. Israel is obliged to keep God's statutes and observe his laws. In doing so, the nation has the task of proclaiming God's truth. Israel's role is to be a prophet to all the nations. Yet despite such an obligation, the Bible asserts that God will not abandon his chosen people even if they forsake this task and violate the covenant. 'I will not reject them,' God declares in the Book of Leviticus. 'I will not spurn them, neither will I abhor them so as to destroy them utterly and break my covenant with them: for I am the Lord their God' (Lev. 26.44). Such a conviction has sustained the Jewish people from biblical times, yet modern history – and most notably the events that took place during the Nazi regime – has challenged this traditional conception of God's concern for his people.

The Problem of the Holocaust for Jewish Theology

Throughout Europe Jews were rounded up in market places, forced into trains, and shipped eastward. The horrors of this process have been depicted in numerous accounts. Crowded together, Jews travelled to their deaths as the pace of murder accelerated. As a local Pole, Stanislaw Bohdanowicz of Zwierzyniec, later recalled in his testimony, the trains carrying these victims were horrifying:

> The small windows were covered with planks or lots of barbed wire, and in some places planks were missing from the walls, which was proof of desperate struggles taking place inside. Through the cracks in the planks and through the wired-up windows peered scared human faces. (Gilbert, 1987, p. 413).

On arrival at the camps, Jews were ordered out of the train and separated into groups. According to a survivor at Treblinka, women and children were sent to the left, men to the right. Abraham Krzepicki testified:

> The women all went into the barracks on the left, and as we later learned, they were told at once to strip naked and were driven out of the barracks through another door. From there, they entered a narrow path lined on either side with barbed wire. This path led through a small grove to the building that housed the gas-chamber. Only a few minutes later we could hear their terrible screams, but we could not see anything, because the trees of the grove blocked our view. (Gilbert, p. 437)

At Treblinka, the women on arrival were shaved to the skin; their hair was later packed up for dispatch to Germany. At the Nuremberg Tribunal one of those who survived, Samuel Rujzman, gave an account of this procedure:

> Because the little children at their mothers' breasts were a great nuisance during the shaving procedure, later the system was modified and babies were taken from their mothers as soon as they got off the train. The children were taken to an enormous ditch; when a large number of them were gathered together they were killed by firearms and thrown into the fire. (Gilbert, p. 457)

The most horrible of all horrors were the gas chambers. The records of the Nuremberg International Military Tribunal reveal in shocking detail the sights within the gas chambers. An eyewitness to the killings at Belzec later recounted a typical occurrence:

Stark naked men, women, children and cripples passed by ... SS men pushed the men into the chambers ... Seven to eight hundred people in ninety-three square meters. The doors closed. Twenty-five minutes passed. You could see through the windows that many were already dead, for an electric light illuminated the interior of the room. All were dead after thirty-two minutes. Jewish workers on the other side opened the wooden doors ... The people were still standing like columns of stone, with no room to fall or lean. Even in death you could tell the families, all holding hands. It was difficult to separate them while emptying the room for the next batch. The bodies were tossed out, blue, wet with sweat and urine, the legs smeared with excrement and menstrual blood. Two dozen workers were busy checking mouths they opened with iron hooks ... Dentists knocked out gold teeth, bridges and crowns with hammers. (Gerstein, 1945)

Where was God amid such horror? Judaism affirms that God chooses the Jewish people, watches over them, and guides them to their ultimate destiny. The questions must be asked then: Where was God when six million died? Where was he when Jewish men, women and children travelled in crowded trains to their deaths? Where was he when wives were separated from their husbands and children from their parents on arrival? Where was he when babies were torn away from their mothers' breasts and machine-gunned in the woods? Where was he in the darkness of the gas chambers? Where was he when bodies were shovelled into crematoria? Where was God at Chelmno, at Auschwitz, at Treblinka, at Sobibor, at Majdanek, and at Belzec?

For over 50 years this dilemma has haunted Jewish thinkers. The novelist Elie Wiesel, an Auschwitz survivor, wrestled with such searing questions in his autobiographical novel, *Night*. He describes his despair in the camps. As he explains, religious doubt set in as he experienced the horrors of the Nazi regime. Describing scenes of terror, he portrays the evolution of his religious protest on the eve of Rosh Hashanah, the Jewish New Year:

> 'Where are you, my God?' I thought angrily, 'compared to this afflicted crowd, proclaiming to you their faith, their anger, their revolt? What does your greatness mean, Lord of the universe, in the face of all this weakness, this decomposition, and this decay? ...
> Why, but why should I bless him? In every fiber I rebelled. Because he had thousands of children burned in his pits? Because he kept the six crematories working night and day, on Sundays, and feast days? Because in his great might he had created Auschwitz, Birkenau, Buna, and so many factories of death? How could I say to him: 'Blessed art thou, eternal, master of the universe, who chose us from among the races to be tortured day and night, to see our fathers, our mothers, our brothers, end in this crematory? Praised be thy holy name, thou who has chosen us to be butchered on thine altar. (Wiesel, 1982, pp. 63–6)

Theology after Auschwitz

In the shadow of the Holocaust, many Jews, including rabbis, lost their faith. In *After Auschwitz*, the American Conservative rabbi Richard Rubenstein, for example, argues that it is no longer possible to believe in a supernatural Deity who acts in history. Rather, the Holocaust has demonstrated that such a belief has no foundation. Jews today, he contends, live in the time of the death of God:

> When I say we live in the time of the death of God, I mean that the thread uniting God and man, heaven and earth has been broken. We stand in a cold silent unfeeling cosmos, unaided by any purposeful power beyond our own resources ...

How can Jews believe in an omnipotent, beneficent God after Auschwitz? Traditional Jewish theology maintains that God is the ultimate, omnipotent actor in historical drama. It has interpreted every major catastrophe in Jewish history as God's punishment of a sinful Israel. I fail to see how this position can be maintained without regarding Hitler and the SS as instruments of God's will. (Rubenstein, 1996, pp. 151–2)

Several years ago I published a book, *Holocaust Theology*, in which I explored the writings of Elie Wiesel, Richard Rubenstein and others who wrestled with the religious perplexity of the Holocaust. All their views, I argued, suffer from numerous defects. In particular, I emphasized that one element was absent from their accounts. There was no appeal to the Hereafter. On the basis of the belief in eternal salvation, which has sustained the Jewish people through centuries of persecution, it might have been expected that Jewish theologians would have attempted to explain the events of the Nazi period in the context of a future life. Yet this did not occur. Instead, these writers set aside doctrines concerning messianic redemption, resurrection and final judgement. This, I contended, was a mistake:

It is not surprising that Jewish Holocaust theologians have refrained from appealing to the traditional belief in otherworldly reward and punishment in formulating their responses to the horrors of the death camps. Yet without this belief, it is simply impossible to make sense of the world as the creation of an all-good and all-powerful God. Without eventual vindication of the righteous in Paradise, there is no way to sustain the belief in a providential God who watches over his chosen people. The essence of the Jewish understanding of God is that he loves his chosen people. If death means extinction, there is no way to make sense of the claim that he loves and cherishes all those who died in the concentration camps, for suffering and death would ultimately triumph over each of those who perished. But if there is eternal life in a World to Come, then there is hope that the righteous will share in a divine life. Moreover, the divine attribute of justice demands that the righteous of Israel who met their death as innocent victims of the Nazis will reap an everlasting reward. (Cohn-Sherbok, 1991, pp. 125–9)

On reflection, however, I now believe that a different direction should be taken in considering the tragedy of the Holocaust. Rather than develop a modern eschatological Jewish theology based on the experience of the Jewish people over the centuries, as I did in *Holocaust Theology*, the time has come for a radical revision of Jewish theology. Indeed, this has been the direction taken by others in considering the events of the Nazi period. In an essay, 'Despair and Hope in Post-Shoah Jewish Life', the American Jewish theologian David Blumenthal maintains that the religious implications of the Holocaust must be faced (Blumenthal, 1999, pp. 1–18). What is required, he states, is a theology of protest. Undeniably, human beings were responsible for the Holocaust. Nonetheless, if one accepts the doctrine of divine providence, then God is ultimately responsible for this human calamity. In his view, we must not piously avoid this challenge. According to Blumenthal, God is present and responsible even in moments of great evil. This leaves us, he writes, with a God who is not perfect, not even always good, but who is still our God and the God of our ancestors.

A leading American Jewish theologian, Arthur A. Cohen, adopts a different approach in seeking to reconstruct Jewish theology after the Nazi era. In *Tremendum*, he contends that it is a mistake to long for an interruptive God who can intervene magically in the course of human history. If there were such a God, he states, then the created order would be an extension of his will rather than an independent domain brought about by God's creative love. Thus he writes that God is not directly involved in human affairs. For Melissa Raphael, a British professor of Jewish theology, the Holocaust demands a revision of traditional Jewish thought. In an essay 'When God Beheld God', she states that the patriarchal models of God must be transcended in confronting the religious dilemmas posed by the Holocaust (Raphael, pp. 1999, 53–78). The patriarchal model of God was the God who failed

Israel during the Nazi regime. Drawing on women's experiences in the camps, she seeks to develop a reconstructed conception of God's presence.

For the American rabbi Harold Schulweis in *Evil and the Morality of God*, traditional theodicies are inadequate in a post-Holocaust world. What is now required, he believes, is a radical reconsideration of Jewish belief. Here he argues for what he calls 'predicate theology' in which divine predicates do not refer to pre-existent hypostasized entities lodged in a mysterious subject and claimed as divine. They are instead qualities discovered not invented, tested, lived and sustained by human beings. Hence, he writes: 'Translating "God is love" or "God has wisdom" or "God possesses compassion" or "God makes peace" into "acting lovingly, or acting wisely, or acting compassionately, or making peace is godly" emphasizes the significance of human interaction and responsibility' (Schulweis, 1984, pp. 122–45).

According to another American rabbi, Steven Jacobs, in *Rethinking Jewish Faith*, the Holocaust demands a new theology for the modern Jew. In Jacob's view, it is an error to believe that God acts in history. What is now required, he writes, 'is a notion of a Deity compatible with the reality of radical evil at work and at play in our world, a notion which, also, admits of human freedom for good or evil because he or she could not act' (Jacobs in Cohn-Sherbok and Cohn-Sherbok, 1995, p. 171). Such theological revision is contingent, he writes, upon accepting a notion of God as other than historically and traditionally presented by both Judaism and Christianity. These and other writers have paved the way for a radically new theological approach. Arguably in our post-Holocaust world, we can no longer accept that traditional doctrines of God are valid. Instead, we must reconsider traditional theological belief in the light of the tragedies of the modern age. Hence, rather than endorsing the traditional understanding of God and the unfolding of a future life in which the righteous will be rewarded, as I did in *Holocaust Theology*, I would now advocate a very different approach to the perplexities of the Holocaust.

What is needed today is a new theological framework consonant with a contemporary understanding of Divine Reality. In recent years an increasing number of theologians have called for a Copernican revolution in our understanding of religion: these writers argue that Divine Reality as it is in itself should be distinguished from Divine Reality as conceived in human thought and experience. Such a contrast, they point out, is in fact a major feature of many of the world's faiths. As far as Judaism is concerned, throughout the history of the faith there has been a conscious awareness of such a distinction between God as he is in himself and human conceptions of the Divine. Scripture, for example, frequently cautions against describing God anthropomorphically. Thus the Book of Deuteronomy states: 'Therefore take good heed to yourselves. Since you saw no form on the day that the Lord spoke to you at Horeb out of the midst of the fire' (Deut. 4.5). Again, Exodus 33.20 declares:

And he said, 'You cannot see my face; for man shall not see me, and live. And the Lord said, 'Behold there is a place by me where you shall stand upon the rock; and while my glory passes I will put you in a cleft of the rock, and I will cover you with my hand until I have passed by; then I will take away my hand, and you shall see my back; but my face shall not be seen.'

The Development of Jewish Thought on the Relationship with God

In rabbinic literature, there are comparable passages which suggest that human beings should refrain from attempting to describe God. Thus, the Palestinian teacher Abin said: 'When Jacob of the village of Neboria was in Tyre, he interpreted the verse "For thee, silence is praise, O God" to mean that silence is the ultimate praise of God. It can be compared to a jewel without price: "however high you appraise it, you will undervalue it."' In another Talmudic passage a story is told of the prayer reader who was rebuked by the scholar Hanina. This individual praised God by listing as many of his attributes as he could. When he finished, Hanina asked if he had exhausted the praises of God. Hanina then said that even the three attributes 'The Great', 'The Valiant' and 'The Tremendous' could not legitimately be used to describe God were it not for the fact that Moses used them and they subsequently became part of the Jewish liturgy. This text concludes with a parable: if a king who possesses millions of gold pieces is praised for having millions of silver pieces, such praise disparages his wealth rather than glorifies it.

The latter development of such a view was continued by both Jewish philosophers and mystics. In *The Guide for the Perplexed*, the twelfth-century Jewish philosopher Moses Maimonides, for example, focused on the concept of negative attributes. For Maimonides the ascription to God of positive attributes is a form of idolatry because it suggests that his attributes are co-existent with him. To say that God is one, Maimonides contended, is simply a way of negating all plurality from his being. Even when one asserts that God exists, one is simply affirming that his non-existence is impossible. Positive attributes are only admissible if they are understood as referring to God's acts. Attributes that refer to his nature, however, are only permissible if they are applied negatively. Moreover, the attributes that refer to God's actions imply only the acts themselves.

Like these Jewish philosophers, Jewish mystics advocated a theory of negation in describing God. For these kabbalists the Divine is revealed through the powers that emanate from him. Yet God as He is in Himself is the Ayn Sof (Infinite). As the twelfth-century kabbalist Azriel of Gerona remarked:

> Know that the Ayn Sof cannot be thought of much less spoken of, even though there is a hint of it in all things, for there is nothing else apart from it. Consequently it can be contained neither by letter nor name nor writing nor anything. (Cohn-Sherbok and Cohn-Sherbok, p. 171)

Similarly, the medieval mystical work the *Zohar* asserts that the Ayn Sof is incomprehensible. It is only through the sefirot (divine emanations) that the Divine is manifest in the world. According to the *Zohar* even the highest realms of the Divine should be understood negatively.

Here then is a new theological framework, deeply rooted in the Jewish tradition, which can serve as a basis for a new vision of Jewish theology in the modern age. Acknowledging the limitations of human comprehension, such a way of unknowing reveals that there is no means by which to ascertain the true nature of Divine Reality. In the end, the doctrines of Judaism must be regarded as human images constructed from within particular social and cultural contexts. Thus, the absolute claims about God as found in biblical and rabbinic literature should be understood as human conceptions stemming from the religious experience of the Jewish nation.

On the basis of this revised understanding of Jewish doctrine, Jewish monotheism, the embracing of myriad formulations from biblical through medieval to modern times, should be perceived as grounded in the life of the Jewish nation. In all cases, devout believers, thinkers and mystics have expressed their understanding of God's nature and activity on the basis of their own spiritual apprehension. Yet, given that God is beyond human comprehension, such a formulation should be viewed as only one mode among many different ways of apprehending the Divine. In this light, it makes no sense for Jews of whatever persuasion to believe that they possess unique truth about God. On the contrary, universalistic truth-claims should give way to recognition of the inevitable subjectivity of all convictions about God.

The same conclusion applies to Jewish beliefs about God's revelation. Instead of declaring that God uniquely disclosed his word to the Jewish people in the Hebrew scriptures as well as through the teachings of rabbinic sages, Jews should recognize that their Holy Writ is simply one record among many others. Both the Written and Oral Torah have particular significance for Jewry, but this does not imply that these writings contain a uniquely true and superior divine disclosure. Instead the Torah, as well as rabbinic literature, should be conceived as a record of the spiritual life of the nation and testimony of its religious quest: as such it should be viewed in much the same light as the New Testament, the Qur'an, the Bhagavad Gita and the Vedas. For the Jewish people their own sacred literature has special significance, but it should not be regarded as possessing truth for all humankind.

Likewise the doctrine of the chosen people should be revised. As I have noted, in the past Jews believed that God had chosen them from all peoples to be the bearer of his message. Although Jews have derived great strength from the conviction that God has had a special relationship with Israel, such a belief is based on a misapprehension of Judaism in the context of the religious experience of humankind. Given that God transcends human understanding, the belief that he selected a specific people as his agent is nothing more than an expression of the Jewish people's sense of spiritual superiority and impulse to disseminate its religious message. In fact, however, there is simply no way of determining if a single group stands in a unique relationship with God.

Again, this new approach to Judaism challenges the traditional conviction that God has a providential plan for the Jewish people and for humanity. The belief that God's guiding hand is manifest in all things is ultimately a human response to the universe. It is not, as Jews have believed through the centuries, certain knowledge. This is well illustrated by the fact that other traditions have proposed a similar view of providence, yet maintain that God's action in the world has taken an entirely different course.

The Jewish conception of the Messiah must also be understood in a similar light. The longing for messianic deliverance should be perceived as a pious hope based on both personal and communal expectations. Although this conviction has served as a bedrock of the Jewish tradition since biblical times, it is inevitably shaped by human conceptualization. Thus like the other doctrines in the Jewish tradition, it is grounded in the experience of the Jewish nation and has undergone a variety of reformulations in the course of the history of the nation. But because God is beyond human comprehension, there is simply no way of ascertaining whether the belief in a personal Messiah is valid.

Again, the same conclusion applies to the Jewish doctrine of the afterlife. Although the belief in the eschatological unfolding of history has been a central feature of the Jewish heritage from rabbinic times to the modern period, it is simply impossible to determine whether these events will in fact occur in the future. In our finite world, limited by space and time, certain knowledge about such spiritual issues is unobtainable. Belief in an afterlife in which the righteous of Israel will receive their just reward has sustained the Jewish people through suffering, persecution and tragedy, yet such a doctrine can be no more certain than any other elements of the Jewish religious tradition.

The Relationship with God Today

The implications of this shift from the religious absolutism of the past to a new vision of Jewish theology are radical and far reaching. The various branches of modern Judaism have advanced absolute, universal truth claims about the nature of the world – but given the separation between our finite understanding and God as he is in himself, there can be no way of attaining complete certainty about the veracity of these beliefs. God transcends human comprehension, and hence it must be admitted that the tenets of the Jewish religion are in principle no different from those found in other traditions – all are lenses through which God is conceptualized. Judaism, in its various forms, like all other world religions, is built around its distinctive way of thinking and experiencing the Godhead.

On the threshold of the third millennium then, Judaism stands on the verge of a new awakening. The way is now open for Jews to formulate a complete reorientation of the Jewish faith. I now return to the initial problem I outlined at the beginning of this chapter. The tragedy of the Holocaust is a religious challenge to Judaism because of traditional assumptions about the nature of God. In the past Jews believed that God chose the Jews for his special purpose. As the Passover liturgy relates:

He brought us out of Egypt.
He cleft the sea in two and brought us through on dry land.
He fed us with Manna and bestowed the Sabbath on us.
He brought us to Mount Sinai and gave us the Torah
He led us into the Land of Israel.

The Passover prayer book admonishes us:

> It is our duty to thank, to praise, to laud, to glorify, to exalt, to commend, to bless, to extol and to acclaim him who performed all these miraculous deeds for our fathers and for us. He brought us forth from bondage to freedom, from anguish to joy, from darkness to great light, from servitude to redemption. Let us therefore sing before him a new song: Praise ye the Lord. Hallelujah.

Such sentiments are based on assumptions about the nature of God: He is the creator of the universe, all-good, all-powerful, and merciful. The Holocaust is an overwhelming problem for Jews because it appears to undermine such convictions. Yet, an acknowledgement of the inevitable subjectivity of religious belief can liberate us from such a struggle. The tragedy of the Holocaust is an overwhelming religious perplexity because Jews perceive God as omnipotent and benevolent, a loving Father of all. However, if God lies beyond human comprehension, then the puzzle of God's providence during the Holocaust ceases to be an insoluble problem. Instead, it is an unfathomable mystery.

This is the message of the Book of Job. In the 38th chapter God thunders forth declaring that his ways are mysterious, beyond human understanding. Therefore Job should remain silent in the face of mysteries he cannot comprehend:

> Then the Lord answered Job out of the whirlwind:
> Who is this that darkens counsel by words without
> knowledge? ...
> Where were you when I laid the foundation of the earth?
> Who determined its measurements – surely you know!
> Or who stretched the line upon it?
> On what were its bases sunk,
> or who laid its cornerstone,
> when the morning stars sang together,
> and all the sons of God shouted for joy?

Or who shut in the sea with doors
when it burst forth from the womb;
when I made clouds its garment,
and thick darkness its swaddling band,
and prescribed bounds for it,
and set bars and doors,
and said, 'Thus far shall you come, and no farther,
and here shall your proud waves be stayed'?
(Job 38.1–11, RSV)

Bibliography

David Blumenthal, 1999, 'Despair and Hope in Post-Shoah Jewish Life', *Bridges: An Interdisciplinary Journal of Theology, Philosophy, History, and Science*, 6:3/4, pp. 1–18.

Arthur Cohen, *The Tremendum: Theological Interpretation of the Holocaust*, Continuum, 1997.

Dan Cohn-Sherbok, 1991, *Holocaust Theology*, London: Lamp.

Dan Cohn-Sherbok and Lavinia Cohn-Sherbok, 1995, *Jewish and Christian Mysticism*, Leominster: Gracewing.

Kurt Gerstein, Statement of 6 May, 1945, International Military Tribunal, Nuremberg document PS-2170, Tubingen.

Martin Gilbert, 1987, *The Holocaust*, London: Harper Collins.

Melissa Raphael, 1999, 'When God Beheld God: Notes Towards a Jewish Feminist Theology of the Holocaust', *Feminist Theology*, 21, pp. 53–78.

Richard Rubenstein, 1996, *After Auschwitz*, Indianapolis: Bobbs Merrill.

Harold Schulweis, 1984, *Evil and the Morality of God*, Detroit: Hebrew Union College Press.

Elie Wiesel, 1982, *Night*, New York: Bantam Books.

3

Islam and the Question of a Loving God

MONA SIDDIQUI

During a lecture to a group of Catholic students in Rome two years ago, I was asked by a young nun, 'How do you Muslims know God loves you?' I asked her how she knew God loved her, to which she replied, 'Jesus died for us, that is how I know God loves me, his only son died for our sins.' This young nun spoke with such conviction about her own beliefs and seemed to be genuinely sceptical as to how Muslims understand God's love with no distinctive event to reflect this love. For her, what God might say in scripture was not enough, it was what God had done to himself to show love for his creation that mattered. This conversation has been one of several in which I have sensed that many Christians understand the concept of divine love as a central difference between Islam and Christianity. Not only is this often understood by clustering Islam and Judaism together against Christianity as religions of the law, more concerned with right practice than right doctrine, but this approach is further confirmed by acknowledging that while Judaism, Christianity and Islam are monotheistic traditions that speak of God's love, it is Christianity alone that speaks of God's unconditional love. The argument is that in Islam and Judaism the kind of love that is manifested through the fulfilment of precepts and submission to God's will is called *nomos* and by its very nature speaks of a bilateral commitment between man and God (Abrahamov, 2003, p. 5). In these two religions, despite the plurality of words that command an affinity between

God and his creation, there is no defining moment when God seals his love for human beings. In whatever ways the ordinary believer understands their relationship to God in daily piety, the scriptural language of love is different in all three religions.

Divine Love in Jewish Scripture

In Judaism and Islam, scripture and prophecy act as God's intervention in human history. Prophets and scriptures bring them something of the divine and their mission is contained within a series of events which mark a renewed existence when humanity once again turns towards God. A relationship of divine calling and divine love is essential to this renewal. But the manner of God's love has been expressed in various ways within the three faiths. In biblical and post-biblical Judaism, love is the principal axis in the relationship between God and Israel. God's specific love for the people of Israel is described in the prophetic book of Hosea. In the *Shir HaShirim* (*Song of Songs*), God is depicted as a husband or lover, not as a Father. In Isaiah 43.1, 4, God says, 'Oh Israel, fear not, for I will redeem you ... and I love you (*Ahavtichah*)'.

For some the core commandment of Judaism is Leviticus 'Love your neighbour as yourself' (Lev. 19.18). Others have stressed various passages in Deuteronomy which served as the most significant sources for many later authorities. The German Jewish philosopher Franz Rosenzweig argues that this commandment to love one's neighbour arises out of the unique love God has for the children of Israel, and that the centrality of this love is reflected most poignantly in:

> Hear O Israel, the Lord is our God. The Lord is one, you shall love the Lord our God with all your heart, with all your soul and with all your strength. (Deut. 6.4–5)

However, Rosenzweig also finds it remarkable that throughout the Torah, God demands that Israel love him but never professes love for Israel except in a future sense; for instance, if Israel loves God, he will bless them in return. Love for God is expressed through carrying out the commandments. This kind of love, *nomos*, sees the cause of Israel's love for God appearing as God's request:

> And now Israel what does the Lord your God require of you but to fear the Lord your God, to walk in all his ways and to love him (Deut. 10.12).
> If you shall keep all these commandments to do them, which I command you this day, to love the lord your God and walk ever in his ways (Deut. 19.9).
> But take great care to do the commandment and the Tora to love the Lord your God (Joshua 22.5). (Fisch, 1998)

Abraham is the best example of such love but here again observing the law is not seen as a way of acquiring God's love but showing love for the divine. The believer loves that which comes from God and that is why he studies the Torah. It is said that in the Seder Eliyahu Rabba, a midrash dating from the tenth century, if the gentiles were able to understand the profound meaning of the Torah, they would love God, that it was due to their love for God that Israel was ready to accept the burden of keeping the commandments (Vajda, 1957, p. 51). Elsewhere it is said that God will imbue the heart of the believer with love and awe of him. Sometimes what is emphasized is that the believer should love God spontaneously without expecting a reward. The *Mishna* in *Avot* says 'be not like servants who serve their masters for the sake of receiving a reward; instead be like servants who serve their master not for the sake of receiving a reward. And let the awe of the Heaven be upon you (*Avot*, chapter 3, in Abrahamov, p. 7).

Divine love which manifests itself as God's unconditional love for his creation is the central theme of Christianity, often encapsulated in 1 John 4.8, 'God is love.' The principal motif of the New Testament is *agape*, God's love for man. This is not a mutual or dialogical love premised on human activity, worship or worth but a love in God for man irrespective of human conduct. Most of all it is a love reflected in the presence of God in Jesus. Jesus' salvific role is based on a love that graced the world because God loved his creation first. Loving one another is an expression and extension of this divine love.

Love in Islam

In the Christian story, Jesus' birth, life, death and resurrection tell a story of divine love which is structurally different to the Islamic story. In Islam, prophecy and scripture are inextricably tied to divine communication so that it is principally through Muhammad and the Qur'an that Muslims come to see God as a moral and eschatological reality. There is an understanding that throughout history God sends and humanity receives different forms of God's communication. It is in this receiving that humankind understands something of God, a God who both hides and reveals of himself. Scripture is given first and written second. By contrast scripture and prophecy play a secondary role in Christianity in the sense that through Jesus Christ, God no longer offers us a prophetic message pointing to an eschatological reality, but rather offers himself; the Incarnation is central to Christian theology. All of God's past wagers on previous prophets and messages culminate in this final act of his self-giving in the hope that 'they all shall know me' (Jer. 31.31).

It is important to note here that although Islamic thought does not have the richly complex theological equivalent of the Christian doctrinal debates such as Resurrection, Trinity and Incarnation, it has an inner story of God which has been lost to some extent in the modern preoccupation with prescriptive obedience. If theology at its simplest level is a fundamentally human attempt to understand God, then the various intellectual disciplines of Islam: speculative theology (*kalām*), philosophy (*falāsifa*), jurisprudence (*fiqh*) and mysticism (*tasawwuf*) are therefore all examples of ways in which human beings articulate their relationship to God. They are all ways of reflecting upon God, his will and his nature. The intellectual response to God is no less than worship itself because belief in God demands an obligation to talk of God; silence, even contemplative silence is not enough. I am reminded here of the last part of Socrates' *Phaedrus* and the comparison between a painting and the written word:

> The painters' products stand before us as though they were alive, but if you question them, they maintain a most majestic silence. It is the same with written words; they seem to talk to you as if you were intelligent, but if you ask them anything about what they say, from a desire to be instructed, they go on telling you the same thing forever. (McAuliffe, Walfish and Goering, 2010, p. 13)

It is up to the exegetes to give voice to this 'majestic silence'. Christianity and Islam have their distinct interpretative traditions but the reception of the divine word is different for each. The most intellectually challenging but spiritually absorbing approach lies in the understanding and reception of God's love. In Christianity, God's love is not confined to scriptural passages alone but reveals itself in Jesus himself. Scripture is secondary to the event of Christ's life and death. The Incarnation is the mystery of the divine taking on human form and thus becoming the essential structure at the very core of a Christian understanding of God. Jesus' role is salvific whereas Muhammad's role is prophetic. The structure and manifestation of God's love in Christianity is fundamentally different from that in Islam. As for scripture itself, the biblical narrative of God's love is dramatic and not just poetic. When one looks for similar verses of God's love for humanity and his creation in the Qur'an, they can appear quite different, even timid in comparison with their biblical counterpart such as the love narrative in John's Gospel. Maybe the most surprising thing is that in the Qur'an there is no commandment to *love* God like the Gospel commandment, 'You shall love the Lord your God with all your heart, and with all your soul, and with all your mind, and with all your strength' (Mark 12.30).

The Qur'an contains various words used for love which define all aspects of human love and divine love. The most common word for love is *hubb* from the verb *habba*, which encapsulates the different dimensions of human desire and divine love. Here, there is no effort to keep the boundaries between *eros* and *agape* as distinct kinds of love; the sacral is reflected in the profane. A persistent theme in the Qur'an is the reflection on human desire for this world rather than the next world. This is reflected both in human desire to prefer the earthly life and also in the desire for the wealth of earthly life:

> Those who love the life of this world more than the Hereafter, who hinder (men) from the path of God and seek therein something crooked. They are astray by a long distance. (Q14:3)

The word is also used for specific things in our earthly life that we should love and that which we should not love:

> Those who love to see scandal spread among the believers, will have a grievous penalty in this life and in the Hereafter: God knows, and you know not. (Q24:19)

The notion of *hubb* is also used to depict different forms of love between people; it can be used to convey false affection:

> Ah! You are those who love them, but they do not love you though you believe in the whole of the Book. When they meet you they say, 'We believe,' but when they are alone, they bite off the very tips of their fingers at you in their rage. Say: 'Die in your rage, God knows well all the secrets of the heart'. (Q3:119)

But the word is also used consistently to refer to God's love for believers and for certain qualities among the believers. In this way, *hubb* is used frequently to describe God's love and those who receive God's love:

> God loves those who keep themselves pure. (Q2:222)
> Do good for God loves those who do good. (Q2:195)
> Say, 'If you love God, follow me for God will love you and forgive you your sins. God is most forgiving and most merciful. (Q3:31)

The word *hubb* and its derivatives are also used for the love that God will not show to humanity. There are a variety of human ills that are not loved by God. These ills can range from denying God and rejecting faith to wasting and squandering:

> God will deprive usury of all blessing, but blesses charitable acts with multiple increase. He does not love the wicked sinner. (Q2:276)

God loves but God can also withhold that love, yet how we experience this withholding is not explored in the Qur'an. When the Qur'an wishes to denote friendship or affection between people, it uses the noun, *mawadda*:

> It may be that God will grant love between you and those whom you (now) hold as enemies. (Q60:7)

The word *mawadda* is not confined to any specific kind of love nor love that is specific to any group of people. It is a sentiment which can be granted by God to human beings or which human beings may feel for each other. The noun *wadd* is also used as in 'On those who believe and do righteous work, God will bestow love' (Q19:96) and 'He is the Forgiving, the Loving (Q85:14).

Revelation is the core of both the Christian and Islamic traditions. How we respond to revelation says something about our relationship to God but also about God himself. The Qur'anic God is intimately but not openly tied to the lives of his creation. God retains the element of secrecy of self by speaking only through inspiration or from behind a veil, never revealing himself directly to humankind. The secrecy motif is presented throughout the Qur'an in various ways: God hides and reveals; God knows the secrets of our hearts but human beings do not know the secrets of God:

> To God belongs all that is in the heavens and on earth, whether you know what is in yourselves or conceal it, God calls you to account for it. (Q2:284)

And he is God in the heavens and the earth. He knows your secret and your disclosure and he know what you earn (by your deeds). (Q6:3)

Whether you keep secret your saying or say it openly and aloud, he knows full that which is hidden in the breasts. (Q67:13)

The multiple verses that refer to chest (*sadr*) or heart (*qalb*) as the places where secrets lie have as an underlying theme God's knowledge of all things human and human inability to keep any secret in the reality of divine omniscience. God sees, watches and hears in the Qur'an and the sense of his panoptic gaze is encapsulated most eloquently in the Prophetic saying that '*ihsan* is to worship God as if you see him, for if not, to know that he sees you'.

When God does choose to reveal to his prophets and messengers his secrets or that which is hidden (*al-ghayb*), they speak clearly about this to their communities even though they announce that they are only the bearers of the message; they have no knowledge of the unseen:

Say, 'I do not say to you, I possess the treasures of God, nor do I know that which is hidden/unseen nor do I say to you I am an angel. I follow only that which has been revealed to me. (Q6:50)

This concept of the unseen or the realm of the unseen (*al-ghayb*) is reiterated in the Qur'an for God has the keys to the unseen (*mafātīh al-ghayb*). But even though God is the unseen who sees all, his love for creation cannot be revealed in its fullness on this earth; it remains veiled. But the fundamental difference is that in Islam, neither God's relationship with humanity nor his love for humanity is dependent on self-revelation or sacrifice of self or sacrifice of another. God remains veiled or hidden; his presence remains in the realm of the unseen transcendent. God wishes to respond from this other realm but he is not a distant God for the Qur'an says that God knows the secrets of our hearts and that he is nearer to us than our jugular vein (Q50:16).

The Qur'anic discourse on God's love demands that we turn to God in prayer, in humility, and in recognition that only God can forgive and that God will forgive. It is replete with a soteriology fixed on divine forgiveness. Human freedom inevitably means human sin but remembrance of God leads to forgiveness by God, however many sins are committed. God's love in the Qur'an is contained in the multiple verses relating to God's mercy or *rahma*. The following is one of the most famous Qur'anic verses to evoke the eternal mercy of God:

> Say, 'Oh my servants who have transgressed against themselves, despair not of the mercy of God for God forgives all sins: for He is oft-forgiving, most merciful. (Q39:53)

There lies a mystery in this overwhelming mercy which while containing within it the sense of compassion is not to be equated only with a forgiving pardon by a superior Creator towards an inferior creation. It is rather a desperate plea from God to humankind not to despair of God's steadfast love in a relationship of ongoing reciprocity. Mercy unlike love is not bilateral in that human beings cannot have mercy on God. But even though it is God who shows mercy, it is also God who desires that human beings draw near to him by asking for his mercy:

> God the Almighty has said, 'Whoever shows enmity to a friend of mine, I shall be at war with him. My servant does not draw near to me with anything more loved by me than what I have made obligatory upon him and my servant continues to draw near to me with supererogatory works so that I shall love him. When I love him I am his hearing with which he hears, his seeing with which he sees, his hand with which he strikes and his foot with which he walks. Were he to ask (something) of me, I would surely give it to him; and were he to ask me for refuge, I would surely grant him it.' (Ibrahim and Johnson Davies 1976, no. 38, p. 119)

The following Prophetic saying describes poetically the spacious-
ness of God's mercy but it also reflects the feminine aspect of
divine mercy:

> And according to a tradition, truly God possesses a hundred
> mercies. From these, he has put away ninety-nine beside himself
> and revealed only one mercy in this world. By virtue of it people
> show compassion to each other and the mother is compassion-
> ate to her child, and the beast is humane with its offspring. On
> the day of resurrection God will join this mercy to the ninety-
> nine and will spread them out over the whole of his creation
> and every single mercy will be in conformity with the heavens
> and the earth. (Al-Ghazālī, 1992, p. 132)

By implication God's blessings too are an extension of his love
even though the word love is not specifically mentioned:

> He gives you from all which you ask him for and if you were
> to count the blessings of God you would not be able to number
> them. (Q14:34)

The Qur'anic verses on love are not concerned with sacrificial or
redemptive love, for the Qur'anic story is different. In Christianity
human beings became alienated from God through the decisive
event of the fall; humanity needs to be reconciled with God but
humanity cannot achieve this on its own or through good works,
rather humanity needs to be transformed in its very essence. In
the Christian faith it is not so much what we do, but what we
are, which needs God's intervention through his loving presence
in the atoning death and resurrection of Jesus. In Islam there is
no equivalent fall and our earthly destiny is not a punishment
but must be regarded as the beginning of our moral awakening.
Humanity has already been forgiven but it is not our essence but
our actions on this earth that matter. Human beings will always
have the propensity to do wrong and thus God remains near to
man, but he does not become man for there is no reconciliation
required, only divine forgiveness.

The Message of Love in Sufi Poetry

While Qur'anic verses emphasize worship and devotion to God through good deeds, it is these same Qur'anic verses which inspired the exuberant flow of Sufi poetry, a poetry where love for God is all consuming. For the Sufis, love is the central theme of our existence in which human and divine love are inextricably intertwined. Some of the most inspirational religious poetry expressing the search and love for God as the only reality, not just an idea, is to be found in the medieval poets of the Islamic world. These poets often used the language of intoxication in their love and search for God:

I am not of this world or the next. Nor of paradise or hell am I, my place is the placeless, my trace is the traceless. I have no body or soul, 'cause I belong to my Beloved entire whole. I have cast aside duality and embraced Oneness. One I seek, One I know, One I see, One I call. He is the first, He is the last, He is the external, He is the innermost. I know naught but Him within, without. Drunk with love, I've lost track of the two worlds. (Jalaluddin Rumi in Jamal, 2009, p. 140)

I swear by Allah that the sun never rose nor set except that each breath of mine was infused with Your Love. I never spoke to friends alone and in every gathering You were the subject of my speech. In happiness and sorrow I did not think of anything but that which You had whispered to me. Nor did I hope to drink in thirst until I saw Your reflection in the cup. (Mansul Hallaj in Jamal, p. 31)

The fire of Your Love is best inside the soul and the soul burning with Your love is best of all. One who has tasted a drop of Your wine today is happy drunk and dazed till judgement day. When You came to be I was hidden; in the beloved's presence, it was best not to be. Give me pain, and cure me not of my Love, 'cause your pain is better than any balm. Since none hope to meet You in this life, this hopeless search for You is best of all. Without You, I am witness to dry autumn. In such an eye, the rain of tears is best of all. Like a candle in separation from You, its best that Attar weep all night. (Fariduddin Attar in Jamal, p. 67)

Despite the passion of such poetry where the only path to God is the path of love, the Sufis did not advocate indifference or negligence of law and piety. Many were jurists and theologians as well as poets, and the foremost theologian of the Islamic world, al-Ghazālī (d.1111), considered both love and law to be central tenets both of Islam and of being a Muslim. Al-Ghazālī's works contain some of the most beautiful and systematic accounts of piety, worship and knowledge of God but al-Ghazālī does not see any conditionality in the prior fulfilment of the law but rather sees observance of the law as the sublime way to show love for God. For al-Ghazālī, love is the inclination of one's nature to something that is pleasant. If that inclination is strong, it is called passionate love and the ultimate pleasure for human nature is God. The opposite of love, which is hate, is a natural repulsion to objects that give pain. Pleasure and pain are the underlying bases of the instinctive human emotions of love and hate, and it is knowledge of objects which gives occasion for either loving or hating. God possesses all the necessary requirements to be the object of a person's love so that knowledge of God is synonymous with love of God. Without knowing God it is not possible to love God.

Al-Ghazālī does not offer any heavy exploration of the Qur'anic language and concepts on love though he mainly uses the word *hubb*. He begins by describing the mystical states and stations towards God and concludes that the love of God is the highest in rank and the last stage in drawing towards God before repentance and patience. Love is not a means to God; love is the end station, for the acquisition of the love of God is the end. He emphasizes that loving God and loving the prophet are compulsory, and that the meaning of faith is love for God and his prophet above anything else. Al-Ghazālī, like Augustine, stresses that real love is love of God, not love of self:

The ultimate rule of perfection of the servant of God is that the love of God Most High triumph in his heart, so that his totality is engulfed (by that). If it is not this, well, it should be more dominant than the love for other things. Coming to understand the true nature of love is so difficult that some of the scholastic theologians have denied it and have said: 'It is not possible to love a person who is not of your kind. The meaning of love is obedience and nothing else.' Whoever thinks this way has no inkling of the basis of religion. (Salam, 2002(b), p. 15)

For al-Ghazālī therefore, love of God 'is the most exalted of the stations; indeed, the objective of all stations is that.' (A *station* is something that is 'permanent and endures' whereas a *state* is to be considered transitory. Salam, p. 15.) Those who love God are perfect servants and this love should engulf the totality of one's person – or at least be the dominant aspect of one's personhood. For some, love of God is impossible because we cannot love that which is totally beyond us, that which is totally transcendent. For al-Ghazālī, the scholastic theologian's position that 'the meaning of love is obedience and nothing else' is wrong; such thinking is reflective of someone who 'has no inkling of the basis of religion' (p. 15).[1] This obedience is to be understood as obedience to the law for:

> The essence of knowledge is to know what obedience and worship are. Know that obedience and worship are conformity to the Lawgiver as regards commands and prohibitions, in both word and deed. (Mayer, 2005, p. 22)

Al-Ghazālī is quite clear that love of God means something more than mere obedience while equally insisting that Muslims must be obedient. For al-Ghazālī, the Qur'an sent as a mercy by God to human beings is proof that God loves his creation. He considers the reward for those who are deemed by God to be law-abiding

---

1 See also p. 38 in which he describes the scholastic theologians as 'the escort of the belief of the unlettered' and being useful for warding off heresy but ultimately lacking in sight.

to be the gaining of knowledge that aids the heart in its perennial battle between appetence and anger thus helping it attain a state of asceticism and detachment from the world:

> And he [i.e. the Messenger] said: 'God Most High floods the heart of whoever eats of the lawful for forty days, without the admixture of anything unlawful, with light and opens the eyes of wisdom in his heart.' One (version of the) Tradition has it that: 'It cuts off the love of the world from his heart.' (Salam, 2002(a), p. 8)

The intimacy of law in relation to God is such that Muhammad is presented as saying, 'Worship has ten parts; nine of those are the seeking of the lawful' (Salam 2002, p. 8). It is possible to say that seeking knowledge of the un/lawful is considered by al-Ghazālī to be not only a form of worship, but also *the most important* aspect of worship. For, when one knows *and does* the lawful, one's heart is filled with light and wisdom which will help form the correct character of the intellect, thus determining one's eschatological horizon. This formation helps encourage worldly detachment and orientation toward the divine. While al-Ghazālī maintains that seeking and doing the lawful result in wisdom from God which helps form the heart correctly, he simultaneously seems to ascribe a higher importance to love:

> The ultimate rule of perfection of the servant of God is that the love of God Most High triumph in his heart, so that his totality is engulfed (by that). If it is not this, well, it should be more dominant than the love for other things. (Salam, 2002(b), p. 15)

Conclusion

How does this love enter us? Like most Sufis, al-Ghazālī does not dwell too much on God's love for human beings. The concept of love for al-Ghazālī bears one meaning when applied to God and another when applied to man. If God's eternal love refers to his eternal will, it means giving man the possibility or the power to come near to God. If his love refers to a divine act then it means unveiling that which creates a barrier between man and God so that man can see God in his heart. As Abrahamov summarizes:

> What al-Ghazālī is actually saying is that God's love for man is the cause of man's love for him, a notion reminiscent of the *agape* motif. If God did not give man his graceful assistance, man would not love him. The signs of man's love for God also derive from the signs of God's love for man. (Abrahamov, 2003, p. 84)

Despite the overlapping importance of acts of worship with inner and outer paths of love for God, the Islamic tradition in the end keeps us forever wondering to whom God will reveal his mercy. For me, this means in the end that despite all knowledge of right action and good deeds, what God really wants is for humankind never to lose hope in him. Again al-Ghazālī offers some of the most beautiful traditions on this topic:

> It is related on the authority of Masrūq that one of the prophets was prostrating himself and an apostate trod on his neck, so that the pebbles adhered to this forehead. So the prophet raised his head in rage and said, 'Be off with you and God will certainly not pardon you.' So God revealed to him, 'You are taking my name in vain in respect of my creatures. Surely I have pardoned him.'
>
> It is related that there were two devotees equal in devotion. When they entered the garden, one of them was elevated to the highest degree over his companion. So he said, 'O Lord in what way did this man exceed me in devotion on the earth? Yet you have elevated him over me in the highest heaven.' So God says, 'Truly, while he was on this earth he was constantly asking for the highest degrees, while you were asking for salvation from the fire. So I have given every creature his request. And this is a pointer to the fact that worship which is on account of hope is

the more meritorious because love dominates the person who hopes more than it does the one who fears.' (McKane, 1962, pp. 21–2)

In Islam, exegetes of all disciplines saw the real story of human relationship to God as one that lay in our love and search for God. God desires this search, he wants human beings to look for him, to worship him, to love him, despite all our weaknesses and sins along the way. The Qur'anic verses of damnation may be terrifying but they are eclipsed by the messages of hope and salvation in the presence of God, best encapsulated in the Prophetic saying about God, 'My mercy prevails over my wrath.' We may not all have the passion and longing of the Sufis in our love for God but in the end that is not what matters. It is the struggle, the often flawed journey towards God, however prosaic or poetic, that God desires and in which we find God's love.

Notes

For a more detailed exploration of the Qur'anic vocabulary of love, see Siddiqui, 2012. For a more detailed analysis of prophecy, love and law in Christianity and Islam, see Siddiqui, 2013. For more on the concept of secrecy and revelation see Khan, 2008, Chapters 1–2.

Bibliography

Binyamin Abrahamov, 2003, *Divine Love in Islamic Mysticism*, Oxford: Routledge.

Al-Ghazālī, Abū Ḥamid Muḥammad b. Muḥammad, *Iḥyā' 'Ulūm al-Dīn*, Damascus: ālim al-Kutub, 1992.

Harold Fisch (ed.), 1998, *The Holy Scriptures*, Jerusalem: Koren Publishers, Jerusalem.

Ezzedin Ibrahim and Denys Johnson Davies (trans.), 1976, *An-Nawawi's Forty Ḥadīth*, Damascus: The Holy Koran Publishing House.

Mahmood Jamal (ed. and trans.), 2009, *Islamic Mystical Poetry*, London: Penguin Books.

Ruqayya Yasmine Khan, 2008, *Self and Secrecy in Early Islam*, Columbia: University of South Carolina Press.

Tobias Mayer (trans. and introduced by), 2005, Al-Ghazālī, *Letter to a Disciple (Ayyuhā 'l-Walad)*, Cambridge: The Islamic Texts Society.

J. McAuliffe, B. Walfish and J. Goering (eds), 2010, *With Reverence for the Word*, Oxford: Oxford University Press.

William McKane, 1962, *Al-Ghazālī's Book of Fear and Hope*, Leiden: Brill.

Muhammad Nur Abdus Salam (trans.), 2002(a), *Al-Ghazālī, On the Lawful, the Unlawful and the Doubtful*, Illinois: Great Books of the Islamic World Inc.

Muhammad Nur Abdus Salam (trans.), 2002(b), *Al-Ghazālī, On Love, Longing and Contentment*, Illinois: Great Books of the Islamic World Inc.

Mona Siddiqui, 2012, *The Good Muslim: Reflections on Classical Islamic Law and Theology*, Cambridge: Cambridge University Press.

Mona Siddiqui, 2013, *Christians, Muslims and Jesus*, New Haven: Yale University Press.

G. Vajda, 1957, *L'Amour de Dieu dans la Théologie Juive du Moyen Age*, Vrin: Paris.

4

The Question of God: Ethical and Epistemological Criteria

DAPHNE HAMPSON

The theme for the St Wilfrid lecture series to which I was most kindly invited to contribute was 'The Question of God?'. How we should conceptualize God is of course the fundamental theological question. I shall consider the criteria, positive and negative, that should inform us in this endeavour. The criteria are both ethical and epistemological (conforming to the truth of the matter). Put in negative terms, ethically we should surely rule out ways of speaking harmful to human flourishing. This is a theological, not simply an 'imported' secular criterion: if God is by definition good, we should not conceive of God in ways incommensurate with this. Epistemologically, the negative criterion must be that we should not speak of God in ways incompatible with what today we know to be the case. If we are to have integrity, we must needs be all of a piece, both ethically and epistemologically. Putting the criteria positively, ethically it is imperative that we conceive of God using metaphors that enhance human well-being. Epistemologically, we should seek to conceptualize God in a manner commensurate with that experience on account of which we find ourselves compelled to speak of 'God'. I shall argue that Christianity falls foul of both these ethical and epistemological criteria. Though I shall primarily consider Christianity, there is good reason to think that other world religions do no better. That this is so uniformly the case of religions raises profound questions as to their provenance and the intent of those who formed them. We are moreover confronted with the imperative of finding new thought forms and imagery to express that which is God.

We should commence with a definition of Christianity. To be Christian is to believe that, in the events surrounding Jesus of Nazareth (to cast our definition as widely as possible), there was present a uniqueness. Classically this uniqueness has been expressed by saying that the second *persona* of a triune God was incarnate in Jesus of Nazareth, Christ being in two natures, fully God and fully human. But the claim that a uniqueness occurred in history may be otherwise expressed. The earliest Christian confession of faith was the adoption of the term ICHTHUS, in Greek an acronym for 'Jesus Christ God's Son Saviour'. Christians claimed this of none other. Meanwhile the book of Revelation refers to Christ as alpha and omega. Again, subsequent to the Enlightenment, given that the classical 'Greek' mode of expression seemed obsolete, there have been attempts to find alternative ways to express uniqueness. Thus Friedrich Schleiermacher, the great liberal theologian of the nineteenth century, spoke of Christ as possessed of an unclouded God-consciousness. While Rudolf Bultmann, the radical theologian of the twentieth century, contended that it is in responding to the preaching of the resurrection of he who died upon the cross that we are delivered into authenticity. But Christians have always known that it is of the essence of their faith to claim that a uniqueness has occurred. Christianity concerns not simply Christ's faith but faith in Christ. An atheist, or a Gandhi, may well venerate Jesus' teaching, but that on its own does not make one Christian.

I shall commence by considering why epistemologically the Christian claim is so improbable, continue by discussing its ethical dubiety, and finally (the more difficult task) attempt to give some indication as to how we might otherwise conceptualize that which is God. (For a detailed consideration of this last, readers should see Hampson, 1996/2002, Chs. VI and VII.)

Epistemological Considerations

In considering the epistemological claims that have been adduced for Jesus' uniqueness it is important to set them in the historical context in which they were advanced. Taking for granted what most of us do in the West (more particularly in Europe) today, we underestimate the depth of the revolution that the European enlightenment represented, making it difficult to conceive of how our ancestors thought. I would suggest that we now know beyond reasonable doubt that there can be no uniqueness such as that which earlier generations claimed for Christ. (At the risk of stating the obvious, we are not here of course speaking of 'uniqueness' in the sense in which we are each unique, but of a uniqueness *in kind*; the uniqueness that Christians claimed for Christ when, in the face of the Enlightenment, they spoke of 'the scandal of particularity'.) We have come to recognize that nature and history form an inter-related causal nexus; that is to say that things belong to categories, are one of a type (though, as we have known since evolution became evident, nature is slowly evolving); while events are part of a sequence of events in a network of cause and effect. To say this is not to imply determinism. Whether or not Caesar crossed the Rubicon it is conceivable that he should have done so, in that there is a class of things, related to other events, called crossing rivers. (If Caesar crossed it, presumably he exercised free will in so doing.) Again, upon seeing a green beetle we take for granted that it is the offspring of like green beetles; it could be no unique example.

Now the Christian claim is not straightforward to adjudicate. For Christian orthodoxy is not that Jesus was a god, one of a kind, but that this person in his full humanity was, in one *persona* (or entity), conjoined with divinity. (Whether being human necessarily precludes being divine is another question, not here our concern; historically this has been a matter of dispute.) The question that concerns us is whether one human being, and one alone, could be possessed of a second and divine nature; and thus be qualitatively other. There is of course no problem in thinking Jesus one among others in the history of the world who have been deeply open to

God. Again, Christians have advanced the claim to a uniqueness having occurred in conjunction not with incarnation but resurrection. But once more, could it be that one man alone has been raised from the dead (not least a biological impossibility)? Among Tibetan Buddhists there are reported cases of a master's disciples after his death having a near-physical awareness of his presence. But if this is what happened in the case of Jesus' disciples, then any claim to uniqueness falls away. Crediting such a possibility, in relation both to Jesus and a Tibetan master, is simply to extend the circumference as to what a person believes (potentially everywhere and in all times) possible. The claim to Christ's uniqueness came about in a world that lacked our modern recognition that there is a regularity to nature, a nexus of cause and effect. All kinds of miracles, or interventions, were thought to occur (as indeed is still the case in much of the non-Western world). In the Patristic period, in which Christian dogma was formed, so much different were people's presuppositions than are ours that the apologist Origen, arguing in the third century for Christ's virgin birth, sets it in the context of other examples (*Against Celsus*, I, 37); while, writing in the early fifth, Augustine sets Christ's resurrection in the context of other comings-back-from-the-dead which had occurred in his diocese (*The City of God*, XXII, 8).

Furthermore it should be pointed out that our knowledge of the wider context has changed dramatically. Those who spoke (at least metaphorically and in some sense literally) of God having 'sent' his Son, thought our world at the centre of the universe, the apple of God's eye, while time was held to go back a mere 6000 years. Talk of God as being 'outside' or 'before' all else seemed meaningful; such that it could be affirmed that, for all eternity, the Son was one *persona* of a triune God, that through him the world was created, who in the fullness of time was incarnate in Jesus of Nazareth. But this talk of 'before' and 'outside' bears no correspondence to how we think of reality today. In terms of scale, we know our sun to be a star part way out in a spiral of a galaxy called the Milky Way, composed of roughly a hundred thousand million stars; and astronomers now think there to be roughly a hundred thousand million galaxies. Time and space are conceived of by physicists as interchangeable, as are matter and energy, such that (however oddly this strikes the non-mathematician) it makes no sense to think in terms of an 'edge' to the universe nor of a 'beginning' to time. (The Big Bang is a singularity to which all tends, not a 'beginning' in a sense often falsely construed, so that it could make sense to speak of 'outside' space or 'before' time.) Nor does it appear that quantum physics, with its suggestion of unpredictability at the sub-atomic level, is an aid to Christian apologetics. Newtonian physics still holds true at the level at which we live; while a resurrection is not a quantum effect but a biological impossibility. Rather than making desperate attempts to fit Christian metaphysics with what we now know, would it not be better to recognize it as respecting the world in which it was created?

In considering the truth of the matter it is enlightening to ask what consequences would follow were Christian claims correct. We should have to say that everything, since the Enlightenment, that we have come to think the case is mistaken. It is not as though an exception could be made to the regularity and inter-related nexus of history and nature. A historical particularity, if true, would bring down the house. But how likely is it that all we have adduced about the nature of the world is false? Putting this in moral terms, why would God (conceiving of God as do Christians as a moral agent) make such fools of us? I have been writing a book on the Danish thinker Søren Kierkegaard (Hampson, 2013), the bicentenary of whose birth falls in 2013. Understanding only too well the challenge with which, subsequent to the Enlightenment, Christian contentions were confronted, Kierkegaard advocates faith in the face of reason. Yet it becomes apparent that, writing in the 1840s, he still holds to pre-modern presuppositions that make incarnation appear at least thinkable. Lacking any real sense for a world of cause and effect, he conceives God to be very directly behind all 'change', such that just about anything can transpire. In nineteenth-century terminology, Kierkegaard is a 'supernaturalist' not a 'naturalist'. Again, he apparently conceives of reality in terms of figuralism, a 'figure' repeating itself in history in an ever-increasing crescendo; such that, foretold in the

Hebrew scriptures, Christ is incarnated in history, which is in turn proleptic of a future consummation. Within such a world view the idea of incarnation could find its place.

Ethical Criteria

I turn to the ethical criteria that we should bring into play in considering how best we may envisage that which is God. Here I should say something that, until one has considered it, may strike readers as extreme. I am persuaded that Christianity is a form of fascism. I take it that the definition of fascism is an ideology the *raison d'être* of which (whether recognized or, as in the case of Christianity, going unrecognized), is to make it look only natural that one part of humanity is superior, or normative for what it is to be human, having the effect of casting those who do not possess these characteristics into the position of 'the other'. Thus National Socialism (as indeed all forms of racism) is rightly held fascist, in that Aryan humanity was declared 'the master race', casting Semitic persons into the position of 'the other'. (One may think that their holding themselves normative or superior on the part of those who do this, serves to consolidate self-esteem. That there be an 'other' is necessary to their self-understanding; in which case anti-Semitism was not incidental to National Social- ism.) In the present context I am suggesting that those ideologies that are the world's religions are calculated to make it look only natural that male is normative, while woman is cast into the posi- tion of 'the other'. That this is the case does not necessarily rule out the possibility that religions have served as vehicles that, in however distorted a form, have carried people's awareness of that which is God.

The mystery is why it should be that half of humanity should have created the symbolic structures that are the world's religions. As the French psychoanalytic thinker of the last generation Jacques Lacan put it, 'the symbolic' (by which he intends lan- guage, culture, and one may think supremely those symbolic structures that are religions) is male. It is as though men have projected a whole symbolic order which, addressing their needs and fears, embodies their dreams and aspirations. Thus we may note that the Father–Son relation – so critical and so difficult of reso- lution for men within a patriarchal, perhaps within any, society – has been a major theme of Western religion. The relation of the 'sons' (a group from which women are excluded) to a transcend- ent 'male' God forms the basic axiom of Judaism. In Christianity, the Father–Son relation is taken up into and resolved within the Godhead. It is, furthermore, difficult not to conclude that the legitimization of male super-ordination over women has been a master theme of Abrahamic religions. These religions are, in an overt manner, masculinist: God depicted metaphorically through the exclusive use of male metaphors. At a covert level, they could well be thought to serve as a palliative designed to overcome the pull of the mother. Exalting the male (in a Freudian understand- ing the third term that interrupts the symbiosis of mother and son), they denigrate women. What these religions notably lack is symbolism that depicts an interchange between man and woman, male and female, conceived of as equals.

Thus God (considered absolute) is gendered male, depicted metaphorically through terms for eminent males in the society in which they are employed for God: 'Lord', 'King', 'Judge', within Christianity 'Father'. Nor is it simply a question of language. The paradigm though which God has primarily been conceptualized is one of his being set over against humanity, characterized through his contrast with humanity; thus omnipotent, omniscient, and omnipresent. Most interestingly God is held to have aseity, to be *a se*, complete in himself, needing none other. It is a mind-boggling projection of what, in his wildest dreams, the patriarchal male might aspire to be. It has been shown that the image of God held by many boys conforms quite closely to this paradigm. But not only theirs: I once heard an eminent, supposedly liberal Anglican the- ologian remark 'when God created he needed to take into account nothing else whatsoever'. God becomes a self-enclosed monad. Of course, there are counter-themes present in the Abrahamic religions, within Christianity notably that of God's *kenosis*, or self-emptying, in the incarnation. But this is a corrective within what continues to be a hierarchical paradigm. It does not convey plurality in equality; certainly not between female and male. Rather is a gender polarity superimposed on the divine/human dichotomy, woman, or the female, being the lower term.

Such a gendering of the divine/human hierarchical dichotomy occurs once and again in the tradition. We may think it both to have reflected gender relations within society and in turn to have served to consolidate gender hierarchy. Consider the book of Hosea. JHWH's relation to the people of Israel (deemed to have gone astray) is compared to Hosea's relation to his wayward wife Gomer (said to have prostituted herself). The 'male', transcendent God forms the lynchpin. It is taken for granted that Gomer should obey Hosea, as should Israel obey JHWH. In Christianity the church (the people of God) is gendered 'female' in relation to Christ the bridegroom. Indeed humanity is personified by a woman, the Virgin Mary, representing within Catholicism the highest to which humanity can attain in relation to the 'male' God. In Islam too, one may think men take on a 'female' subordinate position, prostrating themselves before the more abstract (but still 'male' and certainly not 'female') transcendent God, while they in turn are the masters of women. At the bottom of the heap, women (as in Hosea, but this theme is widely present in the Hebrew prophets) have tended to be associated with the earth or that which is counted unclean, sexual and sinful. Associating himself with the higher, spiritual, term presumably enables man to dissociate himself from a sexuality that he fears, projecting the sexual onto woman. Nor is such a male fright at woman's sexuality confined to primitive tribes. A captain of the North Sea oil industry told me that in the early days men didn't want women present on rigs lest they should be menstruating, fearing this would bring bad luck.

A telling indication that an over-riding purpose of religion has been to legitimize male superiority must be the regularity with which men have superimposed a sacred re-enactment on roles that, in the society, belong to women. Perhaps this arises from a fear of, and so an attempt to undermine, woman's perceived power. Thus every man is born of woman. Symbolically this is reversed as Eve is wrought from Adam's rib, while Athena springs from the head of Zeus. Typically in society it is women who prepare food, and woman can nourish from her body. But the Eucharist or other sacred meals are commonly presided over by men. Women undertake the everyday toil of washing and cleansing. But it has normally been men who have undertaken the rite of baptism. Giving birth has frequently been held to make a woman unclean; until quite recently the Anglican prayer book had a service for the 'churching' of women. While the first, natural, birth has been thought to pollute a woman, men have found it necessary to superimpose a 'second' birth of baptism, through which an infant is 're-born' as a member of the sacred people that is the church. Woman is thus pre-empted by a higher, sacred plane, calculated to undermine her. The instances are too many, their occurrence too widespread, to be mere chance.

While actual women are emasculated, the male ideal of 'the feminine' as pure and untouchable, a figment of his imagination, is placed on a pedestal. Challenged as to the place to which they have assigned woman in their religion, becoming hot under the collar men will frequently point to their veneration of the Virgin, or assure one of the esteem in which they hold their mother. But this represents an evasion of the need to recognize actual women as adult human beings belonging to the neighbouring sex. For woman as a person of equal worth, men have substituted a concoction of their imagination. In Christianity, the images of woman as 'mother' and as 'virgin' (in either case what woman ideally represents for man) have been synthesized in an extraordinary figure contriving to be both. 'The feminine' may indeed be adulated, exemplifying, as Mary responds to the Father God in obedience and humility, what humanity should attain to. Many a man may in effect be saying he finds such qualities lacking in the male world. But the cat is out of the bag when a self-assured woman, presuming to be the person whom she is accustomed to be in the secular world, is told that she is axiomatically debarred from leadership in the religious sphere. The major icon of Christendom depicting the sexes in their relation the one to the other has been that of woman *qua* mother, the all-important baby boy seated on her

knee. Why import what was in origin pagan iconography depicting Isis and Horus into Christianity? To what male need does it
pander?

Nor does the symbolism of the divine reflect gender equality.
Rather is it that characteristics normally associated with woman, or
the 'female', are predicated of the 'male' God. It is he who becomes
the creator from whom the universe comes forth, who is merciful
and possessed of everlasting arms; a motherly father, but never a
fatherly mother. Once again woman as an individuated, concrete,
acting agent disappears. What man desires 'woman' to be for him is
predicated of the male God. It is in this form that 'the feminine' has
been present in Protestantism (Luther would be a good example),
while Catholicism instantiates woman in a separate and inferior
figure to the 'male' God or Christ. Otherwise within Protestantism
any image of woman lacks. Situated six feet above contradiction,
the minister in his (occasionally her) lonely pulpit proclaims the
male God and his son. To repeat: any symbolism of partnership, of
interchange in equality between man and woman, simply lacks in
the Abrahamic religions. Woman is man's inferior, or that which
in his imagination he would have her be for him.

The Present Crisis

The problem is that a gap has opened up between the moral
values and ethos of our society and the religions we have inherited. Nor can this gap be closed. Christians will say that we must
carry through Paul's triumphant proclamation that in Christ there
is no more male and female (Gal. 3.28). Given his phraseology
and vocabulary, echoing the Septuagint translation of Genesis,
Paul may well be suggesting that in Christ, the Second Adam,
woman's subordination to man (her punishment for the Fall) is
overcome (Stendahl, 1966, pp. 32–3). But we don't need Paul
to tell us of human equality; it should be a moral and ethical *a
priori*, as indeed it has become in the modern world. The problem
remains that the Abrahamic religions are 'historical' religions, in
which it is believed that a revelation has taken place in history

(that there has occurred a historical particularity). On account of this, in these religions reference is constantly made to a past world-order. Of course, it is far from the case that all Christians are fundamentalist, but this is beside the point. Whether discussing pacifism, homosexuality or the relation of women and men, adherents of the Abrahamic religions constantly allude to texts that derive from a society with norms and values other than those we embrace today. The fact that these texts are held sacred, moreover read in the context of worship, lends them potency. Their effect works at a subconscious level where it goes unrecognized; the medium is the message.

In this day and age adherents of the Abrahamic religions, as also those who write text books for schools, assume that women should be searched out in the scriptures that the gender imbalance may be somewhat righted. But this is a misadventure, falsely conceived. Where are these women who enjoy equality to be found? Take the book of Ruth, a popular candidate. It is indeed a story of two courageous women circumventing, rather cunningly one might think, patriarchal constrictions. But what assumptions does that text convey? That women, even that they may eat, are dependent on the bounty of men; that their fate is to be decided by men meeting at the town gate; and that their salvation lies in Ruth's producing a male child. In Islam in recent years Fatima has been over-worked. But she is scarcely equal to the prophet (indeed so little is she known that I may need to tell readers that she is the prophet's daughter). It is not she to whom Allah entrusted a sacred text. Nor does it help to look, for example, to Jesus' teaching. He may have been 'kind' to women, but so what? He was kind to men also. If Jesus is to be judged through his parables he had no clue as to human equality. His characters are exclusively male, performing every conceivable role, the sole exceptions being a woman searching for a lost coin, a widow seeking justice, and ten bridesmaids (Slee, 1984, pp. 25–31). No single parable turns on the need to mitigate the lot of women in that society, or to admit them to the religious duties and rights enjoyed by men. Jesus apparently calls God 'Father' without a qualm. Together with his society, he simply doesn't see the issues.

The question is, why are we teaching this literature to our children? What effect may it have in undermining girls, while encouraging boys to think the world rightfully theirs? There is of course no easy solution. People will say should we then not, on account of Shylock, teach *The Merchant of Venice*? Are we to lose Western culture? But in explicating *The Merchant of Venice* it is more than likely that adults will take the opportunity to address the scourge of anti-Semitism in Western history. Do they equally do this in relation to patriarchy when teaching Jesus' parables? Does the church tackle head-on the gender hierarchy induced and justified in Western society through employing male metaphors for God; or the whole association in biblical literature of woman with sexuality? What relationship does the teaching of religion today (as also its inculcation over generations) bear to the fact that there is still profound sexism prevalent in our society? What would need to shift for me no longer to be called 'love' by every bus driver? From what might be thought trivial (but is indicative), to the serious abuse of women (the two most probably being quite closely related), people are unwittingly blind as to the prevalence of sexism and the role religion has played in its maintenance.

Thus it seems to be assumed that discrimination on account of race, sexual orientation and gender are on a par, outlawed in our present society. In fact people's recognition of sexism lags far behind. Consider this. A footballer is in deep water for apparently, under his breath, referring to another footballer as a 'black cunt'. The problem is conceived to be that this footballer has been associated with a woman's genitals. This is held to be 'racist'. (The footballer concerned is indeed black.) The true nature of the problem is not perceived; the reduction of woman to her genitals – and that to associate a man with a woman's genitals is the most obnoxious thing one could fling at him. Then again we are supposed by law to have equality of employment in this country (from which, significantly, religious associations are excluded). Yet, the pope can be invited to visit, the occasion celebrated with all due pomp and ceremony, funded in part by taxpayers' money. It is not publicly said that he heads a profoundly discriminatory body and that it would be unsuitable for the monarchy or any public figure in their official capacity to have anything to do with him; that at most (given the legislation) it must be a purely private visit – funded by the Catholic Church. What message does this give to women as to how seriously equality of employment is valorised by our society?

Why the discrepancy? Presumably because the biological division that is sex is so fundamental that it is taken for granted that women shall perform different, or inferior, roles and, furthermore, that it is acceptable that they be derided by those of the dominant sex. ('Sex', with its Latin 'se' root, found likewise in section, secateurs etc., denotes the great cutting or division of humanity; race, by contrast, is on a continuum.) We should not fail to recognize that, over millennia, a whole cultural baggage has been projected onto this biological division. Furthermore that in the past it was wrongly assumed that there was only one normative human, the male, and (following Aristotle) that women were defective males; this belief for example lying behind Thomas Aquinas' reasoning that women cannot be priested (*Summa Theologica*, I, qu. 92, reply to objection 1). Religion (as we have seen in the examples adduced above) has played no small part in this heritage, turning woman into a repository of 'otherness'. But such understandings are wearing thin today, changing rapidly as women's opportunities, education and job prospects have been revolutionized. When dragged into the present, religions, their texts and imagery soaked in that past are increasingly counted irrelevant. People have moved on. The problem for inherited religions is that, essentially, they cannot.

Meanwhile it is taken for granted that these deeply masculinist and non-inclusive creeds are the only religious possibility, part of the establishment – in a society that prides itself on being non-discriminatory. Consider the following. A person not wishing a church wedding has as the only alternative (unless Quaker) the register office. In a register office it is not permitted so much as to mention God. Rightly or wrongly we are legislating for gay people to be accorded marriage on equal terms. And when will spiritual persons (as so many account themselves today), who are not Christian, on the most important day of their lives be allowed a markedly spiritual ceremony? Again, looking at Ripon Cathedral's website, I found I had been described as a 'feminist' theologian. I did not ask for this and I find it limiting, boxing me in. Observing that a previous St Wilfrid's speaker had been Richard Harries, I was reminded of a correspondence with him. Harries had asked whether he might append to my essay title in a book he was editing, ': a feminist perspective'. Yes, I responded, if after everyone else's title was placed ': a masculinist perspective'. If truth were told, after my title should have stood ': a gender-inclusive perspective', after the others ': a masculinist perspective'. For I have never evinced the slightest interest in a female God, JHWH with a skirt!

A Spirituality for Today?

What would it be to have a religion, or had it better be called a spirituality, which is free from any postulation of a particularity having occurred in history? A spirituality, moreover, in keeping with the axioms, ethical and epistemological, we hold today. Such a spirituality can be gender-inclusive without further ado. No particular provisions are needed to secure such gender inclusivity, other than that we should commence from our present situation, from our world and our awareness of that dimension of reality that we may call 'God', without making over much reference to the past. A gross misunderstanding is liable to arise at this point. People will say 'but are not all human disciplines historical?' Well of course; if by 'historical' we mean that in every discipline (whether music, physics or ethics) people draw on the past in so far as it remains apposite, true or moral; discarding and creating anew in so far as humanity is possessed of new knowledge, insights or values. Such spirituality or theology would become like any other discipline. It is Christianity that is 'the odd man out' in its having a benchmark in the past on account of its being 'historical' in the peculiar sense of the term. Nor is there reason to deny that past religion has often served as what Kant would have called a 'vehicle', one that has served to carry human spirituality. The vehicle needs discarding, while we must seek out thought forms and imagery to carry what it has conveyed.

This is of course no easy task. In that language goes 'all the way down' it has shaped the religion. Most of us will presumably continue to think in some way in continuity with our Western tradition, drawing on past thinkers or spiritual writings as we may. There is no need to make a wholesale bonfire. But we should, furthermore, consider why it is that we continue to hold to a spirituality, that we may find language and thought forms appropriate to what it is of which we are persuaded. For many who count themselves spiritual (and not simply secular) persons, this presumably had something to do with a conviction that there is – for lack of a better expression – more to reality than meets the eye. They find prayer, or a quiet, loving focus on another, perhaps one in need, to be efficacious. Healing takes place in ways that we can scarcely imagine. Further, it would seem that there is something akin to extra-sensory perception that moves between persons. Of course, if this is true today, then that has always been the case; it belongs to what is possible. Not least, we have considerable evidence that one named Jesus of Nazareth appears to have possessed healing powers, as do some persons today. It is also (interestingly) recorded that on occasion he intuited matters that he could not otherwise have known. Again this is true of people's experience today.

The theological question is how we had best conceptualize what it is that is the case. The first step may well be to conceive otherwise of the self than has been the norm in Western culture. If we think of selves as possessed of what have been called 'hard' ego boundaries, and of human relations as akin to billiard balls bouncing off one another, no wonder we lack imaginative ways of conceiving of God. (Indeed, one might think that God has often been conceptualized as just such a 'masculinist' self; placed up there, over-against us, complete in his aseity.) If, on the other hand, we conceive of the self as having 'porous' ego boundaries (not lacking a centredness in self, but 'centred' in such a way that we are open to what is more than self), then we may well be on the way to sensing and naming that greater reality which is 'God'.

Spiritual practices will be important; as has ever been the case for spiritual persons. We must needs refine the self that we may be attuned. God comes to be envisaged as other than a 'being'. (Whether God may be said to have agency is an interesting question.) Rather is 'God' that on which we may draw, or bring into play, as we live out our lives. We shall need quite other language and thought forms to those to which we have been accustomed.

To sum up. It is clear that the religions we have inherited have failed us at this point. The toll of human misery, particularly on the part of woman who have been counted other than the norm, is past reckoning. It is hopeless to attempt to reform systems of thought rooted in a patriarchal past; they must be fatally flawed. No wonder that Christian Churches are beside themselves; obsessed, precisely, with questions of sexuality and of gender which they cannot solve. For there is good reason to think that gender (in particular the attempt to control women) and fear of human sexuality has been the driving force at the heart of our religious mythologies. So long as those religions persist, the past will be carried forward into the present, sowing the seeds of human discord. Yet it is apparently thought suitable to teach these gender-biased mythologies together with ethics and questions of citizenship in our schools! We need to say clearly that such thought-systems are not worthy of a society that prizes the equality and dignity of all persons. Besides which these symbol systems are no longer credible, wholly out of step with all else that we know – and thus liable to be discarded (as they have been by most Europeans) as irrelevant. What is the more remarkable is that so many people still refer to themselves as in some sense spiritual and not simply secular persons. It is surely this that must be cultivated and accorded respect within our present society. As for the role of theologians, we have everything before us as we attempt to conceptualize what we may indeed think to be the case.

Bibliography

Daphne Hampson, 1996, second edn, 2002, *After Christianity*, London: SCM Press.

Daphne Hampson, 2013, *Kierkegaard: Exposition & Critique*, Oxford: Oxford University Press.

Nicola Slee, 1984, 'Parables and Women's Experience', *The Modern Churchman*, 26, no. 2.

Krister Stendahl, 1966, *The Bible and the Role of Women* (pamphlet) Philadelphia, PA: Fortress Press.

5

Art and Religion in the Contemporary World

DAVID JASPER

The theme of my original lecture on which this chapter is based was the place of poetry and art in our world. Rather than simply repeat the words that I spoke then, however, it now seems more appropriate to offer a meditation on what I said in the light of changes that have taken place both in the wider world and in my own experience since then. For if the ancient truths and wisdom of art and religion change little, and Aeschylus, Sophocles, or Job can still move us to tears, their continuing place as literature in our changing world needs always to be reassessed and reflected upon anew. In order to remain attentive to the still centre we must turn and turn again, not ceasing from exploration but our thoughts and hearts active and alert to that which is ever beyond our comprehension yet still demands our complete attention. In this task, which is crucial if we are to survive in any recognizable human form, art and poetry are not optional extras but absolutely and entirely our first guides, as Virgil was the guide of Dante on all his travels in the spirit, from depth to height.

Thus it may be that we can stand over the abyss and even there we can smile. It is partly, and quite simply sometimes, a matter of calling a halt to the frantic pace at which we live our lives, and a matter therefore of giving ourselves the time to stand and stare. In a more religious term, we may call that contemplation. Does not all great art call us to stop and to give our unhurried attention to things of the greatest importance, even, perhaps especially, amid the endless distractions of each day? Whether it calls us to join with the watch of suffering before the cross with the Mother in the *Stabat Mater*, the watch of wonder at van Gogh's *Starry Night*, or the breathless standing upon eternity as Lear dies with Cordelia in his arms – art recalls us to the deep human need for contemplation that alone allows us to know the timeless moment of the sacred in the material world, what Vladimir Nabokov has called 'the marvel of consciousness – that sudden window swinging open to a sunlit landscape amid the night of non-being' (Nabokov quoted in Danto, 2003, p. 159). It was known most deeply in the lives of the ancient fathers of the desert to the extent that it was said of them that 'while dwelling on earth ... they live as true citizens of heaven' such that 'through them ... Human life is preserved and honoured by God' (Russell, trans., 1981, p. 50).

The Sacred in Literature and Art

In *The Sacred Community* (Jasper, 2012), I focus on that still moment of eternity in the Christian liturgy when the community on earth is one with angels, archangels and the countless host of the faithful past, present and future in the singing of the hymn of praise which is known as the Sanctus and which has its beginning in the vision of Isaiah in the Temple in Jerusalem (Isa. 6.1–3 KJV): 'Holy, holy, holy is the Lord God of Hosts. Heaven and earth are full of your glory.' Here, for one still moment, eternal though in time, we sing of the glory of God even here on earth, on the edge of the abyss, just before the moment when we are turned in the narrative of the Eucharist of the Western liturgy to the moment of betrayal on that one singular night in human history.

It is, we might presume to say, the task and vocation of the artist and poet to call us to a renewed sense of the pressure of glory upon the things of earth. Many years ago, the great American scholar of literature and religion, Nathan A. Scott Jr., truly one of God's trombones (Johnson, 1927, 2008), called us to preserve at all costs a place for the *Literae Humaniores* within the curricula of all studies of religion, reminding us of:

an art that very much wanted to wake the spirit's sleep, to break that somnolence into which we flee from the exactions of the moral life; and it consistently expresses a fierce kind of rage at the feckless, lack-lustre slum to which the human world is reduced when, through indolence of spirit or failure of imagination men [sic] have lost all sense of the pressure of glory upon the mundane realities of experience and have thus 'fallen' into the profane. (Scott Jr, 1969, pp. 272–3)

The form of such language may now seem a little heavy and dated, but the energy and the vision remain vital. Much of my time since 2009 has been spent working and teaching in Renmin University of China in Beijing, surrounded on every side by the fierce competitiveness of contemporary China, and in the heart of a city that is now estimated to be of some 30 million people. It is in this metropolis that I now sit, and here it is all too easy to forget almost everything but the mundane glory of human industry and the pressures of economic growth. And yet, it is here, too, that I have found the still centre of art in the work of the artist Ding Fang, to whom I shall return in a while. Always, if we but take the time and care, there may be moments of reprieve that preserve us finally from that deadly fall into the utterly profane that finally can only usher in upon us the inhumanity of the night of non-being.

I returned to the writings of Nathan Scott, a professor of literature and religion and a priest, whom I liked and deeply respected though rather feared, during a recent time of revisiting the roots of the series of conferences on literature and religion which I and others began in the University of Durham in 1982, and which continue to meet biennially today (Jasper in Sugirtharajah, ed., 2009, pp. 41–53). The conferences gave birth, also, to the journal *Literature and Theology*. The history of these conferences is not our concern here, but as I reflect now upon the scholars of those times, some 30 years ago, I am struck by something that we find all too rarely today in theological studies – that is, a profound religious humanism to be found in the writings that remain from them, a kind of rich density of life and vision that looks back to

Erasmus and the Renaissance and that still found space even in the later twentieth century for the things of the spirit and for the art that holds them before us (see Klemm and Schweiker, 2008, for more recent work in Theological Humanism). This was in an age just before the postmodern turn overtook us in our universities, looking back in England to a time when the Church spoke with a clearer intelligence than, on the whole, it possesses or chooses to reveal today, and when art and literature seemed closer to the heart of the everyday. Perhaps we were more concerned with what we sought to communicate rather than caught by a fascination with the technology of the act of communication. I do not think that I am merely being nostalgic, though I may easily be accused of that. It was also a time, perhaps, when we paid more direct attention to literature and art and less to what was being said about them, to their 'impact' and their immediate, measureable value in our society: it was not just a matter of art for art's sake, but a dwelling in the moment of art that somehow demanded no further justification. The critical turn in the later 1980s to theory and to the criticism of cultural studies had its importance in many ways – an awakening of the conscience into various forms of liberation that was sorely needed – but it was also, in some degree, a turn away from that immediate and close contemplative attention which had once been paid to the deep grammar that lies within and sustains things of lasting worth and beauty, as well as the mysteries of pain and suffering. Art and poetry moved to the surface of things and away from the less-easily articulated depths. Most of those who spoke at those early conferences on religion and literature in the early 1980s had experienced war, or its loss, at first hand, and knew more of the bloodbath that was the twentieth century than those of us who followed after them. It was inevitable that even before the century's end the younger intellectuals who had bathed with a degree of carefree abandonment in the conditions of deconstruction and postmodernity[1] began to know

---

1 We began, Terry Eagleton once remarked, eager to drive a coach and horses through everyone else's beliefs without taking up the inconvenience of holding to any ourselves. But, 'by the late 1980s, card-carrying deconstructionists looked like becoming an endangered species, not least after

a re-awakening once again of the ethical, and to feel the need to find a way back to the language of truth and the spirit. But by then its grammar and the art of the theological was no longer as self-evident as it had once seemed to be, and the artists who were the guardians of the vision, with a few notable exceptions, were either no longer with us, or else were speaking a language that seemed to offer no intelligible space for the contemplation of the things of the spirit. At least, I admit, to me, it seemed harder to find them. No one now, of course, learns the mystery of grammar in school, and few read the classics in their original languages – and that is a pity, or perhaps even more than that. Meanwhile, the Christian Churches, as institutions, speak less and less coherently as they think less and, therefore, except in their celebration of the ancient liturgy, *see* less. But perhaps I am just becoming irredeemably old fashioned.

Nevertheless, if it is indeed a truth that without a vision the people will die, then it is equally the case that without a living memory we quickly forget who we are. Artists are the guardians of both vision and memory, and the art that remains fresh in its defiance of time makes us feel at one with those who have gone before us in history – it thus makes the singing of the Sanctus a genuine 'existential' possibility, even for us. No one who enters the Uffizi Gallery in Florence can fail to be staggered by the overwhelming freshness of great paintings of Botticelli, the *Primavera* or the *Birth of Venus*, seen not in copies but in the flesh, so to speak. They seem to have been created but yesterday, their paint hardly dry, and as we stand in contemplation before them time simply stops.

---

the high drama of the so-called de Man affair in 1987, when the grand master of US deconstruction, the Yale critic Paul de Man, was revealed to have contributed pro-German and anti-Semitic articles to some collaborationist Belgian journals during the Second World War' (Eagleton, 1996, p. 196).

Religion in English Poetry

In English literature we have to go back (and T. S. Eliot was no bad
guide here) to the early seventeenth century and the metaphysical
poets – John Donne and George Herbert above all – to find an
eternal freshness and density of metaphors in an irreducible pri-
macy that was doomed to fade in poetry once the age of reason
began to persuade us that metaphors could be unpicked and the
stuff of poetry could be 'translated' into a language that is more
comprehensible, its 'meaning' abstracted from the fabric of the art.
Romanticism, it is true, gave us something of a complex recovery,
but still without the freshness or the originality. In Germany and
in England, Shakespeare was rediscovered, above all in the genius
of Coleridge and A. W. Schlegel, but he remained their master.
Linking literature and theology, John Coulson, who was one of
our guides in those early conferences, finely remarked that 'in the
poetry of Donne and Herbert, literary adequacy seems to denote a
religious adequacy, and vice versa. Its adequacy is manifested in a
particular *density* of metaphor; and it is this which pre-eminently
characterizes the poetry of the Shakespearean tragedies. It is a
density at once literary and religious' (Coulson, 1981, p. 17).

I have since discovered exactly what he means in teaching
Herbert's poetry to undergraduates. Take the example of perhaps
his most famous poem, 'Love (III)':

> Love bade me welcome: yet my soul drew back,
>   Guiltie of dust and sinne.
> But quick-ey'd Love, observing me grow slack
>   From my first entrance in,
> Drew nearer to me, sweetly questioning,
>   If I lack'd anything.
>   (Herbert in Wilcox, ed., 2007, p. 661)

Here, inextricably and shockingly, we find intermingled the language of Eucharistic devotion, the language of the weary traveller,
and the language of eroticism. They cannot be unbound or the
metaphors unpicked. As Love draws us sinners to the Eucharistic

banquet, the unwilling travellers bringing the dust of the journey, so too this call is the enticement of the lover who draws the timid and retiring lover back to a full erection. Students often find this shocking, the more 'religious' among them often are offended, and that is exactly what Herbert, the benign and beloved priest of Bemerton, wants, though his motive only is love. The metaphors remain in their density, offering a complex grammar of reconciliation which too often we are unwilling to entertain, preferring to reduce Herbert's art by our safer divisions of life into seemingly more manageable sectors and divisions.

One could re-state this in more philosophical terms. It was wisely said to me at the outset of our conferences on religion and literature by my own teacher in Durham University, Professor Ann Loades, that we needed philosophers at these interdisciplinary meetings, to keep us on the right track and to prevent us from becoming too satisfied with our woolly thinking. Our mentor in this respect was the Wittgensteinian philosopher D. Z. Phillips. (It might be remarked in passing that Wittgenstein's late *Philosophical Investigations*, treating of language, the concepts of understanding and of meaning, and of the states of consciousness, should remain compulsory reading for anyone embarking on such a project as mine in this essay.) Phillips reminded us in his lecture at our very first conference that if we abandon proper 'grammatical requirements we shall soon find ourselves engaged in trivialities or nonsense' (Phillips in Jasper, ed., 1984, p. 25). By such requirements he means a proper embedding of what Flannery O'Connor calls the 'mystery' in the 'manners' of everyday life. It is the task of the writer, and indeed of all artists, to reassemble for us, ever and anew, the 'coinherence' (to use a favourite word of Charles Williams) of the ancient and prophetic wisdom of mystery with the stuff of common, everyday life. It is precisely for this reason that all forms of fundamentalism will inevitably fall to dust as they seek to *impose* the one upon the other and thus the density of metaphor is atrophied and lost. Where this coinherence is sustained in art then we are necessarily committed to forms of grammatical precision that keep our vision mediated, and language then acquires the irreducible capacity and energy to enact that very thing which it states. Thus the language of art and literature becomes the medium for an authentic, perhaps even sacramental poetics, a *poiesis* or 'making' and a 'doing in remembrance' in the bringing of the past into the present and a movement towards the as yet unknown future, all drawn into one timeless moment, the doctrinal command given in 1 Corinthians 11.25, and Luke 22.19. In their originality, the poet and the artist draw us to behold even that which God saw in the beginning of his creation when he saw that it was good (Gen. 1.4) – the beauty that resides in the particularities of the commonplace and everyday, the world in a grain of sand, the ever new glories of both the natural and the sublime.

The greatest painters in the Western tradition of art – Rembrandt, Velasquez, van Gogh – hold us in the contemplation of their art to the profound beauty in the faces of the poor, aged and worn, in the everyday things which we take for granted, the domestic pots and pans, the scuffed shoes, all the common stuff of daily life, and it is in them, taught by the artist, that we learn to see and feel the pressure of glory, and participate in the meeting of heaven and earth.

Another way to put this is in George Herbert's phrase, in which we discover 'heaven in ordinary' (Herbert, *Prayer (I)* in Wilcox, p. 178). In art and poetry, Herbert suggests, though himself a preacher, we may find more easily than in many a sermon the mystery that connects us to true, sacrificial liturgical celebration, for, as he says in perhaps the most quoted lines in seventeenth-century poetry:

A verse may finde him, who a sermon flies
And turn delight into a sacrifice.
(Herbert, The Church-porch, in Wilcox, p. 50)

Thus the mystery of the sacrament lies at the very heart of the poetic, linking the often inarticulate business of the everyday and often its very inadequacies with the things of deepest import. If it is an ancient truth that of that which is most sacred we must remain silent, then silence is often found in our struggle for words when no words will do.[2] Such a moment is caught by the contemporary English poet and priest David Scott in a poem that describes a visit that must be, perhaps above all in its quiet sense of failure, familiar to any pastoral carer when faced with the unanswerable questions of life and death. It is a poem of pure understatement, its concern being with the silence that can heal more than any human achievement in a deliberate move from the universal to the acutely particular beauty and tragedy of bereavement. It is entitled simply 'Parish Visit' and is drawn from Scott's own life as a parish priest in rural Westmoreland:

> Going about something quite different,
> begging quiet entrance
> with nothing in my bag, I land
> on the other side of the red painted step
> hoping things will take effect.
> The space in the house is ten months old
> and time has not yet filled it up,
> nor is the headstone carved.
> He died when he was twenty
> and she was practised at drawing
> him back from the brink
> cajoling in spoons of soup.
> We make little runs at understanding
> as the winter afternoon
> lights up the clothes on the rack;
> we make so many
> the glow in the grate almost
> dips below the horizon,
> but does not quite go out.
> It is a timely hint
> and I make for the door and the dark yard,

---

2 See Yarnold SJ, 1973, 'The Disciplina Arcani', pp. 50–4, and Wainwright, 1980, pp. 38–9: 'At times, adoration will pass over the linguistic horizon into silence. Even that silence is directed towards God, and it is qualified by what the stammering tongue has been straining to say.'

warmed by the tea,
talking about things quite different.

(Scott, 1984, p. 77)

Within the stumbling, here unheard, words of care (it does not even matter what they are), a deeper silence is embraced in which it is profoundly necessary both to speak and not to speak. And here, in the inevitable inadequacy of the priestly (the poet Friedrich Hölderlin knew this so well),[3] the poetic knows that it is precisely *not* a matter of arriving at some hidden meaning, but rather of a 'letting the unsayable be unsaid'. (Heidegger quoted in Clark, 2002, p. 118)

It is as we stumble in our cries to God, still willing to believe even in the face of unbelief, that the careful grammar of a deeper kind, that which the poet calls our raid upon the inarticulate (Eliot, 2001, 'East Coker'), makes for us a better sense. It is still profoundly related to all other forms of grammar, linguistic, philosophical, but it is found also in our speechless awe in the face of the beautiful and the terrifying. Such a grammar does not seek vindication or value in any contribution that it may make to forms of organization which are, in the end, but forms of subjection. Rather it constitutes a shift towards the symbolic in its disturbing depths, and thus, inevitably, towards the sacrificial and the sacramental which, to nudge the now familiar language of S. T. Coleridge on the symbol, 'always partakes of the Reality it renders intelligible; and while it enumerates the whole, abides itself as a living part in that Unity, of which it is the representative' (Coleridge, 'The Statesman's Manual', in White, ed., 1972, p. 30). Coleridge, though, in Charles Lamb's words, a damaged archangel, perhaps, is rarely less than precise, and he, too, enunciates here something of the depths of the Eucharistic mystery. In T. S. Eliot's words, the poet, also, is 'constantly amalgamating

---

3 'That I approached to see the Heavenly,
And they themselves cast me down, deep down
The false priest that I am, to sing,
For those who have ears to hear, the warning song.
There ...' (Hölderlin, 'As on a Holiday ...', p. 399); also Mark 4.9.

disparate experience' (Eliot, 1951, 'The Metaphysical Poets', p. 287) to bring us, with the greatest of precision, to the foot of the mystery where all is gathered into one. Such a voice, like the utterances of all great art, speaks with a quietness that calls us to listen, or perhaps to watch, with breathless attention lest we miss a word of its complex web and the sense of unity is thereby dissolved and lost. We have forgotten in our hurried lives, most of us, what it is to listen and to watch, to contemplate, with a patience that does not parade devotion nor strut with meddling intellect, yet is precise in tranquil recollection though humble enough to know its limits as, in Wordsworth's words,

> ... the soul
> Remembering how she felt, but what she felt
> Remembering not, retains an obscure sense
> Of possible sublimity ...
>
> (Wordsworth, 1850, 'Book II', pp. 315–18)

Of Wordsworth's *Prelude*, so closely linked to the life of Coleridge, A. N. Whitehead once remarked with perceptive humility that 'the sheer statement, of what things are, may contain elements explanatory of why things are. Such elements may be expected to refer to depths beyond anything that we can grasp with a clear apprehension' (Whitehead, 1927, p. 115). The privacy of such a comment brings to my mind that most understated, even ordinary, of our poets, (I mean no slight upon his genius) W. H. Auden, quietly attending Holy Communion in Christ Church, Oxford, where his friend Bishop Peter Walker was the celebrant, appreciated precisely because he never intruded his own personality into the words that he spoke with such care.[4]

---

4 'Auden might not parade his devotion, but there are moments when, in terms of his own understanding of things, it must be remembered that he died a communicant member of his church, as I am humbled to remember recalling a Palm Sunday morning Holy Communion (his last) in Christ Church Cathedral, Oxford, at which I was the celebrant' (Walker in Jasper, ed., 1984, p. 59).

The Art of Ding Fang

And so I return to my self-imposed exile in Beijing. In the midst of the city's mad rush there is a pool of quiet in the spirit of the artist Ding Fang. Though he has been deeply immersed in the recent turbulent history of China, Ding Fang's deeper life is lived in a far more profound awareness of the timelessness of the natural world and human involvement with it. His conversation avoids peripheral questions and quietly, insistently, refocuses us on the experiences which his art, in its many forms, calls to our attention. Almost liturgical in its repetitiveness, each image of that art is at once new and a finite repetition of the infinite unchangeable. In this sense, art is always new and, like the Eucharist, unitary – a participation in the one great act. Yet – like the work of such contemporary artists in Europe and America as Anselm Kiefer and Bill Viola, both of whom have commonalities with Ding Fang's work in their universalism – his is an art which resists interpretation through the terms of any one religious tradition. Its metaphorical density, even like that of the seventeenth-century Christian poet George Herbert, is finally too resistant to all attempts at reduction to avoid the shocking, or perhaps better, the living quality which is finally the life of the spirit that is here celebrated. It is never art's task to draw attention to itself or to solve problems in any limited or immediate way, but to remind and to bring us to that life which we then each interpret in our own way. As the poet Wilfred Owen said in the midst of the horrors of the war that killed him: 'All a poet can do today is warn. That is why the true Poets must be truthful' (Owen in Day Lewis, 1963, p. 31).

The focus of Ding Fang's pictures may be upon the simple toils, habitations or journeys of humankind within the minute particularities of Chinese life. Ding Fang is a fine grammarian and a careful draftsman, his art a discipline that is both a gift and is learned. Like those of Rembrandt, his sketches can reveal a moment with fine, almost deceptive simplicity. At the other end of the scale – like a Beethoven who can shake us with a full symphony, the Pastoral or the mighty Ninth, or speak in the deeply personal and complex intimacies of the last string quartets – Ding

Fang can also overwhelm us with huge canvasses which evoke mountains that can only be seen in the particular light of China (he himself notes that the light of Spain or Britain is quite different) and yet are universal in their fixity in creation, heavy with the pressure of glory. In between, perhaps, is the art of the human form, another calling upon our attention – *ecce homo* (see John 19.5) – in pictures of infinite sweetness and muscular strength. Not that at any time can these things be separated, for they are all one.

Ding Fang speaks no English, and I speak no Chinese. We depend upon an interpreter. And yet in our conversations, I sense a commonality which is rare, and it is a special kind of knowing. Words have a profound life of their own apart from the particularities of any language. For my part, as best I can, such knowing is constituted in a listening and a watching; though one which has a particular relaxation to it as it seeks no resolution of understanding, yet, it demands as well an intense and contemplative form of attention. In that sense it is like the reading of poetry or perhaps, dare one say it, the utterance of prayer which is as much a patient listening as a speaking. These conversations between us are rare moments in a teaming city, and in a university – which has been my 'natural' environment for most of my life, a place dedicated, one hopes at least, to learning and the art of hard critical thinking. They are, I think, moments of what I have come to call 'liturgical living', akin to worship but within the everyday (See Lacoste, trans. Raftery-Skeban, 2004, and Jasper, 2012, chapter 1, 'The Biblical and Liturgical Space'). From my reflections on them and on my viewing of Ding Fang's art, I have tried to stand back and express what the experience has been for me. That is rather different from the more usual critical processes of 'reading' literature or interpreting art. Yet some understanding there must be, and, like my own teachers before me, I tell my students time and again that it is only in close and careful readings, in slow attention to grammar and structures of the metaphors, will they begin to hear and see what is being spoken and shown.

Still, in the end, it is in the community which such care alone makes possible that vision and memory become an act of common utterance. What the art and the poetry make present to us is the sudden swinging open of the window or door in moments of revelation that we then must find place for in our common lives and their mutual responsibilities – the answer to the question, what is it all for, its purpose, perhaps. In the Christian Eucharist the narrative must be followed to the bitter end in human history, to fracture and to consumption in betrayal and loyalty. But the Great Thanksgiving begins in creation and finds its unity in the great song of the Sanctus – 'Holy, holy, holy is the Lord God of Hosts. Heaven and earth are full of thy glory.'

That is a supreme moment of the deepest reality, known only under the pressure of glory. It embraces the inarticulacy of David Scott's halting parish visit, the shocking metaphors of Herbert's poetry, the tragic terrors of Aeschylus's *Agamemnon*, or the Chinese art of Ding Fang. Each shares a grammar, perhaps even what Cardinal John Henry Newman would have called a grammar of assent, that is both particular and universal, and universal *because* it is, in each case, painstakingly particular. And this validates, for us, the absolute necessity of the place of art and religion in the contemporary world, and their interdependence not in violence or dogmatisms, but in recognitions of the other, and therefore of oneself in the recovery of holiness and of the vision of heaven in ordinary.

Bibliography

Timothy Clark, 2002, *Martin Heidegger*, London and New York: Routledge.

S. T. Coleridge, R. J. White, ed., 1972, *Lay Sermons, Collected Works*, Vol.
6, Princeton: Princeton University Press.

John Coulson, 1981, *Religion and Imagination: 'In Aid of a Grammar of
Assent'*, Oxford: Clarendon Press.

Arthur C. Danto, 2003, *The Abuse of Beauty: Aesthetics and the Concept
of Art*, Chicago and La Salle, IL: Open Court.

C. Day Lewis, ed., 1963, *The Collected Poems of Wilfred Owen*, London:
Chatto & Windus.

Terry Eagleton, 1996, *Literary Theory: An Introduction*, Second Edition,
Oxford: Blackwell.

T. S. Eliot, 1951, *Selected Essays*, Third Edition, London: Faber & Faber.
T. S. Eliot, 2001, *The Four Quartets*, London: Faber & Faber.
Friedrich Hölderlin, trans. Michael Hamburger, 1994, *Poems and Fragments*, London: Anvil Press Poetry.
David Jasper, 'Nathan A. Scott Jr's The Wild Prayer of Longing', in R. S. Sugirtharajah, ed., 2009, *Caught Reading Again: Scholars and their Books*, London: SCM Press.
David Jasper, 2012, *The Sacred Community*, Waco, TX: Baylor University Press.
James Weldon Johnson, 1927, 2008, *God's Trombones: Seven Negro Sermons in Verse*, London: Penguin.
David E. Klemm and William Schweiker, 2008, *Religion and the Human Future*, Oxford: Blackwell.
Jean Yves Lacoste, trans. Mark Raftery-Skeban, 2004, *Experience and the Absolute: Disputed Questions on the Humanity of Man*, New York: Fordham University Press.
D. Z. Phillips, 'Mystery and Mediation: Reflections on Flannery O'Connor and Joan Didion', in David Jasper, ed., 1984, *Images of Belief in Literature*, London: Macmillan.
Norman Russell, trans., 1981, *The Lives of the Desert Fathers*, Kalamazoo: Cistercian Publications.
David Scott, 1984, *A Quiet Gathering*, Newcastle-upon-Tyne: Bloodaxe.
Nathan A. Scott Jr, 1969, *Craters of the Spirit: Studies in the Modern Novel*, London: Sheed and Ward.
Geoffrey Wainwright, 1980, *Doxology: A Systematic Theology*, London: Epworth Press.
Peter Walker, 'Horae Canonicae: Auden's Vision of a Rood – a Study in Coherence', in David Jasper, ed., 1984, *Images of Belief in Literature*, London: Macmillan.
A. N. Whitehead, 1927, *Science and the Modern World*, Cambridge: Cambridge University Press.
Helen Wilcox, ed., 2007, *The English Poems of George Herbert*, Cambridge: Cambridge University Press.
William Wordsworth, 1850, *The Prelude*, London: Penguin.
Edward Yarnold SJ, 1973, *The Awe-Inspiring Rites of Initiation: Baptismal Homilies of the Fourth Century*, Slough: St Paul Publications.

6

Does Equality Override Religious Freedom?

ROGER TRIGG

Is Religion Important?

Why does religious freedom matter? Does it? Many would say that our democratic freedoms are sufficiently safeguarded by an appeal to freedom of conscience. If it is then suggested that that is merely a freedom for individuals, whereas religion is typically also a community activity, then the right of freedom of assembly is also invoked. What more, it might be said, do religious people want, unless religious freedom is really a form of special pleading? Perhaps the purpose of invoking such freedom is actually to obtain privileges for religious people and religion in general, so as to in effect make non-religious people second-class citizens. A demand for equality between all citizens could easily entail that the state make no distinction between people of different beliefs, or indeed the beliefs themselves.

The state, it seems, should be neutral. Otherwise, some would claim, we are in the same position as if a democracy were to give privileges to, say, Conservatives, that are not given to Liberal Democrats. A true democracy treats all beliefs equally, and privileges no one on the grounds of their belief. This view, coupled with a strong 'liberal' belief in the autonomy of the individual, inevitably results in the state withdrawing to a position of neutrality, not just between religions, but between religion and non-belief. That, in fact, is roughly the position of the French Republic with its policy of *laïcité*.

The neutrality of the state to beliefs goes further than the belief that the law of the land should treat everyone equally. The law can certainly have no favourites. This view drives the state to a 'secular' position that detaches it completely from any championing of particular religious views. In fact, it must mean that the state can stand for nothing, and exists in a moral vacuum. Anything else would immediately put it on the opposite side from the views of some of its citizens. When put like this, the objective is clearly impossible. Even the ideals of freedom and equality, themselves the staples of democracy, are substantive principles that have to be defended and taught to future generations. They have themselves to be justified, and be principles that are grounded in something stronger than the sociological fact that that is what 'we' happen to believe in at the moment. A good case can be made for the fact that these principles are themselves grounded in Christian belief. We are equal because we are all equal in the sight of God. We are made in his image. We should be free because that is a recognition that we have been endowed by our Creator with free-will. Whether this is the only justification that can be given may be controversial, but it is a historical fact that our democratic principles, and those of Europe generally, have grown out of a long history of Christian thought and practice. How long we can retain a vibrant belief in either freedom or equality without the Christian faith that nurtured those beliefs is one of the great questions of our time. It is ironic that, in particular, the belief in equality is being used to marginalize the very religious basis that brought it to life.

This brings us back to the fact that religious freedom is being challenged as a category on the grounds that it is just special pleading or privileges religious believers. Because the typical 'liberal' position is to see personal autonomy as the supreme good, religion can no longer be seen as something good in itself. It is only worthwhile in so far as individuals think it important for their own lives. Religion is a private matter, of no concern in the public square. It is something that consenting adults can choose to do, but it is only important as the expression of individual preference. Religious organizations and public worship are important as a form of voluntary association, just as golf clubs are. In a free society, we have to take account of what they do, but there is no apparent justification, it seems, for rating one person's preferences above another, and certainly no justification for the state coming to any view about the truth or otherwise of beliefs.

We thus are rapidly coming to a point, even in England with its Established Church and long Christian history, where religion is not seen as intrinsically important. This can already be seen in such moves as making the definition of a charity depend on the idea of 'public benefit'. Previously religion (and education) were seen as by definition charitable objects. Now religion has to show its contribution to the public good. That may seem unexceptionable, except that public opinion can be very fickle and can easily come to view some religious standpoints as unacceptable if they are out of step with the fashions of the day. Resistance by Churches to involvement with gay marriage provides only one example of an area where traditional Christian principles and fast-changing contemporary mores become so out of alignment that religious bodies could easily come to be seen as having a malign, not beneficial, effect on society. They might therefore easily be judged as not 'charitable' according to the law.

Issues about religious freedom, whether for individuals or religious organizations such as Churches, must never be decided on the basis of what one agrees with, or even what the majority accepts. Freedom is at its most vulnerable, and also most precious, when the exercise of the religious conscience is at odds with majority opinion. Democracy depends for its functioning on different people bringing their differing judgements and reasoning into the public forum, so that a collective decision can be reached. If there is no room for the lone prophet or the maverick, let alone whole communities and institutions, able to rouse the consciences of others, the fabric of democracy is harmed. If there is pressure to conform, democracy will become fossilized and will perish. When the pursuit of equality results in dreary conformity, freedom itself is at risk.

One reason for singling out religion for special protection may not involve any judgement about its truth. It is just that, of its very nature, it has always proved vulnerable to the exercise of arbitrary authority. All religion posits grounds of transcendental obligation, and sources of authority outside the reach of the state. In particular, a belief in God suggests that human power must always be subject to a higher authority. This is made clear symbolically in the Coronation Service at the beginning of a monarch's reign. It is also symbolized by the cross surmounting the crown. Even the sovereign, and the authority she personifies, are subject, it is held, to a higher law, and under judgement by a higher judge. This symbolism refers to something of enormous importance, namely that the authority of our government, and that of any land, can never be regarded as the ultimate authority. It is subject to moral demands that all governments should recognize. It is no wonder that totalitarian governments that wish to control everything, and that recognize no authority beyond themselves, find such a view repugnant. It is no wonder that totalitarians will always try to control, and even persecute, religions that refuse to accept the State or the Party as having sole ultimate authority. In fact, this battle is still being fought in countries such as China where the Communist government is terrified of losing control over religious movements and demands subservience to an earthly rather than a heavenly power. In such circumstances, the service of God can quickly be stigmatized as unpatriotic.

Freedom of Religion as a Human Right

In contemporary Europe, the ideology of human rights is to some extent being used as an external break on governments to stop them treating their citizens in objectionable ways. In that respect, 'human rights' themselves can take on a transcendental role apart from the policies of governments, which can find appeals to such rights as irksome as the interference of any religious authority. Yet 'rights' are not an acceptable secular alternative to religion, since an appeal to them still does not answer the question why they in turn matter. What is important about freedom and equality, for example? We are immediately taken back to conceptions of human nature, which themselves are likely to have a religious foundation. Saying that we believe in rights because we do, or that they are essential to democracy, does not take us very far in teaching the importance of rights to those who may even wonder whether or why democracy is important.

Another problem with a glib appeal to rights, devoid of any principled belief in their basis, is the simple fact that they conflict. Many of the apparent assaults on religious freedom being made in the name of the law arise because the demands of different rights offer different guidance. It is an old philosophical problem that freedom and equality may each guide us in different directions. If, for instance, we want economic equality, there may have to be restraints by a government on people's freedom to spend their money as they wish. Even taxation is a restriction on freedom. The problem is always how to strike a balance. The same problem arises when the needs of equality and the specific needs of religious freedom conflict.

There can be no doubt that freedom of religion is itself a human right. Some, particularly in the United States, would argue that it is the 'first freedom', not only because it is named first in the First Amendment of a Bill of Rights added to the US Constitution. They would suggest that without religious liberty there can be no real democratic freedom. If we are not free to live according to what we think most important and advocate policies in accord with that, we cannot genuinely and sincerely be able to contribute to democratic debate.

In the European Convention of Human Rights, Article 9 guarantees an absolute right to freedom of 'thought, conscience and religion' and a right to manifest religion or beliefs, which is qualified by, for instance, the need to protect 'the rights and freedoms of others'. Article 14 itself sets up an important marker outlawing forms of discrimination. It holds that the enjoyment of the rights and freedoms set out in the convention 'shall be secured without discrimination on any grounds such as sex, race, colour, language, religion' and other similar factors. Sexual orientation is not specifically mentioned in this Article, but is now recognized as a relevant ground.

It should be clear that there are plenty of possibilities for conflict between different rights, and that, in particular, any accusation of discrimination is liable to be taken seriously enough to override claims to religious freedom. To take the example of racial discrimination, it will hardly be a defence that one's religion encourages it, as the Dutch Reformed Church in South Africa once appeared to do. This is illustrated by a recent case in the new United Kingdom Supreme Court, concerning admission to a Jewish school (UKSC 15, 2009). The problem was how to define who is a Jew. The normal Orthodox Jewish definition is through matrilineal descent. The boy in question was the son of a woman who had converted to Judaism, but not according to Orthodox procedures. The Jewish school, however, applied Orthodox standards of conversion that did not recognize the practice of non-Orthodox Jews. The argument seemed essentially a theological one, and alarm bells should have rung when the judgment of the Court began with quoting Deuteronomy. Nevertheless, the conclusion of the Court was that, in fact, though not in intention, the school was discriminating on racial grounds. That is absolutely proscribed by the 1976 Race Relations Act, and the need not to discriminate had to take precedence over any theology. The decision of the Court was narrowly reached by five to four, and in one of the dissenting judgments, Lord Rodger said 'The decision of the majority means that there can in future be no Jewish faith schools which give preference to children because they are Jewish according to Jewish law and belief' (UKSC 15, para. 225).

This case is interesting in two respects. It illustrates that it is not only Christians who can find that their religious freedom is restricted. It also shows how a charge of 'discrimination' can easily trump any claim to act in accord with one's religious conscience. The current secular priorities of the State can easily take priority. If one looks again at the relevant Article proscribing discrimination in the European Convention, discriminating against someone on the grounds of their religion is itself to be ruled out. Yet it appears all too easy for 'religion' to drop out of consideration in pursuit of the eradication of other forms of discrimination.

One reason for this can be gleaned from various recommendations emanating from the Council of Europe, itself the body that appoints the European Court of Human Rights. There has long been an anti-clerical suspicion of religion in countries such as France and Spain, which may be understandable given their history. Even so, it is liable to creep in to pronouncements that apply to all Europe. For instance in one document we are told that states may 'not allow the dissemination of religious principles which, if put into practice, would violate human rights'. They add ominously that 'if doubts exist in this respect, states must require religious leaders to take an unambiguous stand in favour of the precedence of human rights, as set forth in the European Convention on Human Rights, over any religious principle' (PACE, 2007, Doc. 11298). Nothing could illustrate more clearly the way in which, for some, the State must reign supreme over any religious authority and principle. There can be no accommodation for religious principle. Secular standards have to be applied and respected. This may be in the spirit of the French Revolution, but it is very far from the tradition of respect for religion and religious freedom that has been at the heart of British and American democracy since at least 1689. It is assumed that religions are of their very nature separate from, and even opposed to, human rights. The idea that such rights depend on ideas of human dignity that themselves need a religious base, does not even appear to be on the horizon.

These kinds of pronouncements are all the more curious, because, as we have seen, the right to religious freedom is built firmly into the European Convention on Human Rights. Yet time and time again, it appears to have to take second place to the need not to discriminate. This is even though the paradoxical result may be discrimination against religious belief itself. One way the courts sometimes try to avoid this is by defining the right to religious freedom so narrowly that practices that may appear to be associated with religion are not deemed religious. A right to manifest religion can then be pared down essentially to the right to freedom of worship. Important though this is, it is hard to say that engagement in public rituals is the only manifestation possible of religious belief.

Can Rights Be Trumped?

Courts are not above deciding what is and is not essential for someone's religious belief. For example, a worker may want to wear a
cross, and for various reasons be told not to. In a case concerning
a British Airways employee that was to go on to the European
Court of Human Rights, the Court of Appeal in London said of
the appellant that neither she 'nor any witness on her behalf suggested that the visible wearing of a cross was more than a personal
preference on her part' (EWCA, 2010, Civ. 80, para. 37). They
continued by saying that 'there was no suggestion that her religious belief, however profound, called for it'. Thus something that
may be important for religious reasons to an individual can be
dismissed as mere 'preference'. Unless something was a 'requirement' of faith, it is not seen as a result of faith. Yet, there was more
than a suspicion that the cross was being banned precisely because
it was seen as a religious symbol. Maybe wearing it was a matter
of individual choice, but being forbidden to do so brings in other
considerations. Indeed the judgment refers to problems that occur
when someone holds that a practice adopted by an employer 'con-
flicts with beliefs which they hold but which may not only not be
shared but may be opposed by others in the workforce' (EWCA,
para. 40). Does that mean that opposition by colleagues can justify
restrictions on freedom? It is surely precisely in such circumstances
that individual freedom should be respected.

The European Court of Human Rights eventually found in
favour of Ms Eweida, the British Airways employee. In a significant, but small step, the Court said of her desire to manifest her
religious belief (ECHR, 2013, para. 94): 'this is a fundamental
right: because a healthy democratic society needs to tolerate and
sustain pluralism and diversity; but also because of the value to an
individual who has made religion a central tenet of his or her life
to be able to communicate that belief to others'. In a second case,
however, of a nurse wishing to wear a cross on a chain round her
neck while on duty, the Court accepted that health and safety
concerns might be more important. Religious freedom is still very
circumscribed.

One remark in the original English judgment reflects a curious but pervasive view of religion, namely that it is matter of choice and individual commitment. The case of the Jewish school betrayed a 'Protestant' attitude to religion that seemed unable to grasp any view of religion that failed to stress individual commitment. Religion, despite the evident Orthodox Jewish position, could not be something one is born into. Yet, at least until recently it was a pervasive Roman Catholic position that one would be born a Catholic. Certainly this is the view of Islam concerning its religion. Because one is born a Muslim, one cannot in many countries be allowed to commit 'apostasy' and change one's allegiance to another religion. These views can be criticized because they do not place enough emphasis on individual freedom and, instead, stress the role of the community as a source of one's identity. They go against the individualist emphasis evident in most discourse about human rights. Nevertheless, that does not mean they do not exist as religious beliefs.

In the judgment about the wearing of a cross, reference is made to grounds of discrimination, such as age, race, sex and sexual orientation and so on. These are referred to in the context of legal attempts to enforce equality of treatment for groups that are possibly disadvantaged. 'Religion or belief' is part of the list, but the Court of Appeal neatly distinguishes it from other grounds of discrimination in a way that is clearly intended to devalue it compared with the rest. Lord Justice Sedley said: 'One cannot help observing that all of these apart from religion or belief are objective characteristics of individuals; religion and belief are matters of choice' (ECHR, para. 40). The implication is that one should be respected for what one cannot do anything about, but one must accept the consequences of what one chooses. This makes a mockery of any idea of freedom of religion, since it appears that discrimination on the grounds of religion can be justified on the grounds that individuals need not hold the belief, whereas, for example, someone cannot help being black. Religious people cannot then claim equality of treatment in the way that women or homosexuals can, since, it seems to be implied, they can change their beliefs. Indeed religious persecution has often taken place with that objective, but that is hardly reassuring in this context.

Other judgments also tend to devalue religious belief and accompanying practices in comparison with other grounds of discrimination. As we have seen, one method is to narrow what counts as a genuine religious practice, so that the charge of religious discrimination cannot be properly levied. One long-running case also ended its journey through English courts by being taken to the European Court of Human Rights. It concerned a civil registrar, Ms Ladele, who claimed that she could not conduct civil partnership ceremonies in the London Borough of Islington because of her Christian beliefs. There was no reason to doubt her sincerity or strength of feeling about the issue. She was prepared to lose her job rather than go against her conscience. She happened to be black, and it is interesting that if she had been able to claim that she was being discriminated against for racial reasons, she would have had an easy ride. There was no suggestion of that, but because it was her religious beliefs that came into question she received little sympathy from two courts, after winning the case in the initial Employment Tribunal. Discrimination on the grounds of sexual orientation was seen to trump any idea of religious discrimination.

The judgment in the Court of Appeal by the Master of the Rolls contained the view that 'Ms Ladele's objection was based on her view of marriage, which was not a core part of her religion; and Islington's requirement in no way prevented her from worshipping as she wished' (EWCA, 2009, Civ. 1357, para. 51). Here again we have a remarkably limited view of what religious belief consists in. Freedom of religion is deliberately reduced to freedom of worship. This is combined with an assumption that an English court is well qualified to rule on theological issues, and can say what is and is not a core part of a religion, in this case Christianity. Yet, it is apparent that views on marriage can go very close to the core of Christian belief. St Paul even compares the love of husband and wife to that of Christ and the church (Eph. 5.25). Even so, the European Court of Human Rights (ECHR, 2013) upheld the original decision, making freedom of religion

take second place to discrimination on grounds of sexual orientation. No attempt was made to balance the rights or to seek any
reasonable accommodation between the two. Indeed it remarked
(para. 105) that under its case-law 'differences in treatment based
on sexual orientation require particularly serious reasons by way
of justification'. In other words, freedom of religion carries little
weight when issues of equality and discrimination are to the fore.

The worry in cases like this when individuals take a moral
stand which may not be taken by all, or even most, of those with
whom they share a faith, is that religious freedom can degenerate
into an ability to claim that any practice is 'religious' and to be
protected. Sincerity cannot be the only guide, or others will be
forced to respect whatever I choose to think at the time is important for me. That could include anything. If religious freedom is
to mean anything, there has to be some constraint on what can
count as religious. In the two kinds of cases already mentioned,
this need not be a worry. It may be true that all Christians may
not agree on the need to display a cross or to have nothing to
do with civil partnerships or same-sex marriage. The point is
that both stances are completely intelligible against a Christian
background. The British Airways worker, Ms Eweida, was not
claiming that wearing, say, a shamrock was an integral part of her
faith. No one can dispute the importance of the symbolism of the
cross for all Christians. Similarly not all Christians are opposed
to civil partnerships, and many may agree that discrimination of
homosexuals should be forbidden. Even so, Ms Ladele's moral
stand is clearly one Christian reaction to the introduction of such
a legal relationship, which many saw as the first step to allowing gay marriage. Her views, right or wrong, are firmly rooted in
centuries of Christian moral theology concerning the nature of
marriage. Hers is not an idiosyncratic position, and indeed the
issue continues to cause deep divisions in many Churches.

The courts seem intent on narrowing the definition of what is
to be seen as religious, and also restricting what can be seen as a
'Christian' belief'. As we have seen, that latter step is exception-
ally dangerous for any court, as it involves its making rulings on
what can and cannot count as Christian belief, or at least 'core'

belief. That has to be beyond its competence, just as it should have been beyond the competence of the UK Supreme Court to make decisions that impinged in a central way on Jewish theology. The underlying theme in many law suits, however, and it can be seen most clearly in both the Jewish school case, and the civil registrar case, is that 'discrimination' is so abhorrent that it must be outlawed to such an extent that the exercise of religious liberty can never be an adequate defence. Individuals can demand equal rights, and the pursuit of that equality is deemed so vital, that it has to trump or override every other consideration. This attitude can sometimes be helped by an underlying antagonism towards religion, and the view that religion is itself a harmful influence in society stimulating conflict and division.

Yet, there is no hierarchy among human rights, we are often told. If that is right, and even those who want to give priority to religious freedom itself are mistaken, there is still the question why a right to equal treatment, and not to be discriminated against, can apply to many different kinds of groups but not religious ones. We have already encountered the specious reason that religions are allegedly chosen, so that whether people are committed to one is within a believer's own control. That, however, should not justify discrimination that targets those who have chosen a particular religion. A democracy should not tolerate the persecution of any on grounds that they have chosen a way of life or set of beliefs. Otherwise, the ill-treatment and even persecution of Conservatives by Socialists, or Liberal Democrats by members of the United Kingdom Independence Party (or vice versa) would be perfectly acceptable. Yet, clearly it strikes at the root of all democratic freedom. In the same way, targeting religious groups, even if they are regarded only as voluntary associations, undermines the freedom that has to lie at the basis of all democratic societies.

The European Convention outlaws discrimination on the grounds of religion, and this then has to be balanced against other forms of discrimination. The very worst way of resolving this issue is by appeal to public opinion or the fashions of the day. We are then standing on quick-sands, as public opinion can change with remarkable speed. Unless we surreptitiously begin to give some priority to one form of discrimination over another, there is no way out of the situation but to balance the competing demands against each other, and try to meet both as fairly as we can. All rights matter, and nothing is solved by one trumping another. The watchwords therefore ought be 'reasonable accommodation'. Each side must be given as much as possible without compromising the position of the other. In the case of the civil registrar, Islington council wanted to make a point. They had determined that the protection of gay rights was far more important than respecting a religious conscience. Yet, in fact, they could have easily safeguarded both sets of rights. Islington employed other registrars, and, without any fuss, Ms Ladele could have been given the kind of work that she had already been doing for many years, while other registrars took on the new duty of registering civil partnerships. The service could have been provided, while conscience was respected.

In this kind of case, it is all the more important that conscience be respected when most of us are convinced that the exercise of conscience in question is misplaced. It is easy to accommodate people when we agree with them. What is more crucial – and integral to the nature of democracy – is that people's views and practices are safe-guarded when we do not share them and even violently disagree with them. The exemplar in this regard is that of conscientious objection in time of war. People now generally recognize that it is the mark of a civilized society not to coerce those with deep moral objections into fighting and killing. That does not mean that most people will agree with them, or that they may not be expected to contribute to a war in other ways. They cannot opt out of their obligations as citizens. Nevertheless their moral views, which are intelligible and even admirable, are accommodated. It is the mark of a free society that people can bring differing moral insights into the public arena. At times a small, unpopular minority may even eventually convince the majority that they are right. The enforcement of conformity can only mean the dead weight of totalitarian government and the end of all freedom.

Freedom *for* Religion?

Any democratic society has to strike a balance between the views of its citizens, and this is especially true in the pluralist society in which we live, in which we dare not assume a settled agreement about basic issues. However, we do all have to live together, and enforcing the views of one section of the population on another cannot be the way to do this. Religions have often been accused of doing this themselves, and the spectre of so-called 'theocracy' is often raised. Certainly the example of some Islamic countries is not reassuring. The English tradition, however, has for centuries been very different. 'Nonconformists', first in a religious sense, and latterly more generally, are tolerated, and even respected. Reforms beginning in the seventeenth century have ensured that one does not have to have particular religious views (such as being a member of the Church of England) in order to be recognized as citizen.

The danger now is coming from the opposite direction. Religious people are not trying to coerce others. They do, however, feel increasingly coerced themselves. In the 1960s, a sociological thesis became influential concerning the 'secularization' of society. In particular, it was believed that the advance of science would cause religion to wither away. As a sociological tenet, this has not stood the test of even a few decades. Religion is resurgent in many parts of the world. Not just Islam is growing in influence. Different forms of Christianity are growing exponentially in many areas, such as China, Africa and Latin America. The United States stands as a disproof of the alleged fact that there is a direct connection between increasing scientific knowledge in advanced societies and the withering of religious influence.

Yet, in Western Europe, in particular, it remains true that societies are increasingly indifferent to religion. Sociologists can argue about the causes of this, but it is clearly not inevitable. There is no subtle social 'mechanism', or process, such as may be implied by the word 'secularization'. We are not in the grip of social forces that cannot be resisted. However, many of the attitudes live on, which are bound up with the idea that science will drive out religion. Many assume that science tells us 'the truth', while religion at best is concerned with 'faith'. Faith is then contrasted with reason, which is deemed the province of science alone. Religious belief then becomes a subjective preference, which cannot be justified in the public square. Religion is made a private matter, to be accommodated only grudgingly. The idea that it can contribute positively to discussions about the common good is jettisoned. Faith cannot be dismissed or marginalized on the grounds that it is not a matter of reason, but is a mere matter of taste, and moreover a taste that many do not share. Religions make claims about what is true and deserve to be listened to. They can be argued with and criticized, but for that to be possible they have to be allowed into the public square in the first place. They cannot be dismissed by a quick philosophical definition restricting all reasoning to the confines of science.

These views surface in the law courts and contribute to an inability to take religion in general, and Christianity in particular, seriously. Religious belief is seen as a private, if idiosyncratic foible, outside the range of rationality. It can even be seen as a threat to civil order, because of its controversial nature. It is forgotten that Christian principles, even such fundamental ones as a belief in justice or equality or freedom, have lain at the foundation of English common law and the functioning of our society. Religion cannot, and should not be, sidelined under the influence of outmoded sociological assumptions. Even philosophical beliefs that make science the arbiter of truth cannot be accepted. Science itself always needs a further metaphysical justification (Trigg, 1993). Faith and reason cannot be arbitrarily separated; faith is always faith 'in' something that has to be rationally specified. It must take its chances in the public square, and not be suppressed. The corollary of this is that a religious conscience should not be swept aside, but should, if possible, be accommodated. Discrimination on the grounds of religion is indeed to be deplored, since this is as harmful as any other form of arbitrary discrimination.

When we talk of freedom of religion, two different pictures can govern different people's minds. For some, freedom *of* religion is the aim, so that there is a level playing field, and religion itself receives no privileges. Often it is claimed that this entails the neutrality of the State towards religion, but that can imperceptibly slide into the view that the State must, at least in public, be swept clean of all religious influence. We are sucked into a view that demands freedom *from* religion. That itself entails the privatization of religion, and neutrality can slide into a practical atheism in the conduct of affairs. In a neutral state, it has to be assumed that religion can make no positive contribution to public affairs. That may seem fair, but atheists are likely to feel far more comfortable in such an environment than any religious believer. The latter will be expected to leave all religious beliefs behind when entering into public deliberation. Atheists can, it seems, confidently retain their anti-religious assumptions. Atheists are not penalized for being forbidden to wear a cross, whether in fact or metaphorically. Many Christians are. They are forbidden from putting their faith explicitly into practice.

Another picture remains more sympathetic towards religion, while not assuming it should dominate, and while ensuring that there can be no coercion into religious practices. It accepts that Christianity has been woven into the fabric of England since it first became a recognizable country. Removing Christianity from public view could have incalculable and unpredictable effects on the whole of our society. The heritage of our country is profoundly Christian. Indeed our stress on the importance of religious freedom has itself always had a theological basis. A coerced love of God is a contradiction in terms.

Perhaps what is needed is freedom *for* religion, whereby the potential value of religion for our society is recognized. That entails a more sympathetic view of religion in the courts than appears to be gaining in influence at the moment. It involves seeing discrimination against people on the grounds of strongly held religious belief as dangerous for wider society. It entails a greater willingness to accommodate belief and to strike a better balance between other human rights and the undoubted right to hold a religious belief and to manifest it (see, for example, Trigg, 2007 and 2012).

Bibliography

England and Wales Court of Appeal (EWCA), 2010, Civ. 80, *Eweida v. British Airways PLC.*

England and Wales Court of Appeal (EWCA), 2009, Civ. 1357, *Lillian Ladele v. London Borough of Islington.*

European Court of Human Rights (ECHR), *Eweida and Others v. The United Kingdom*, Strasbourg, 15 January 2013, Applications No. 48420/10, 59842/10, 51671/10 and 36516/10.

Parliamentary Assembly, Council of Europe (PACE), 2007, *Document 11298: State, Religion, Secularity and Human Rights*, online at http://assembly.coe.int/ASP/Doc/XrefViewHTML.asp?FileID=11607& Language=EN.

Roger Trigg, 1993, *Rationality and Science: Can Science Explain Everything?*, Oxford: Blackwell.

Roger Trigg, 2007, *Religion in Public Life: Must Faith Be Privatized?*, Oxford: Oxford University Press.

Roger Trigg, 2012, *Equality, Freedom and Religion*, Oxford: Oxford University Press.

UK Supreme Court (UKSC), 2009, *Case of R(E) v. Governing Body of the Jewish Free School*, online at http://www.supremecourt.gov.uk/docs/uksc_2009_0105_judgmentV2.pdf.

7

God and the Human Person – Faith in the Contemporary World

CATHERINE PEPINSTER

Daniel O'Leary is a Roman Catholic author, a former parish priest of Ripon, and a man with a remarkable talent for summing up the human condition and humanity's relationship with God. In both his various books and his articles for *The Tablet*, he has regularly written of humanity's constant wondering, its desire for something more than itself. 'There is a kind of ache', he wrote in *Unmasking God*, 'for something that is always beyond, a restlessness that never goes away' (O'Leary, 2011, p. 72). We have all felt it, that sense of something just over the horizon, just beyond our reach, and we have sensed it in music and poetry – that reaching out, that desire for the transcendent. The poet Matthew Arnold summed it up in 'The Buried Life':

> But often in the world's most crowded streets,
> But often, in the din of strife
> There rises an unspeakable desire
> After the knowledge of our buried life:
> … A longing to inquire
> Into the mystery of this heart which beats
> So wild, so deep in us – to know
> Whence our lives come and where they go.

Perhaps it was the psalmist who summed it up most succinctly with that most powerful of similes,

Like a deer that yearns for running streams,
So my soul yearns for you my God.

(Ps. 42.1)

That, for Christians – indeed for others too of the Abrahamic
faiths – is what will satisfy the deepest longings of the human
heart – what makes sense of life and where we come from and
where we go. It is God, or, as *Nostra Aetate,* the Second Vatican Council's 'Declaration on the Relationship of the Church to
Non-Christian Religions' put it, it is 'that ultimate and unutter-
able mystery which engulfs our being and whence we take our
rise and whither our journey leads us' (Second Vatican Council,
1965(b), para. 1).

But the Incarnation means that God is not merely a mystery.
When the Brakkenstein Community of Blessed Sacrament Fathers
in Holland wrote their monastic rule they began it by saying:

Brother
You want to seek God with all your life,
And love him with all your heart.

But you would be wrong
If you thought you could reach Him.
Your arms are too short, your eyes are too dim,
Your heart and understanding too small.

But the community went on to reassure their new brothers that it
is the Incarnation of Christ that changes everything:

In Jesus of Nazareth
a man shows
how completely we can belong to God;
how much freedom and humanity
how much courage and self-forgetfulness
a man can possess
when he has been found by God
and has surrendered himself to Him.
In Jesus there is also a future for you.

The community's Rule articulated an assurance, a faith that God is not a distant God but a God who has the most profound understanding of our situation, with whom there is the possibility of relationship, and of transformation of the human condition.

Christianity and the Human Condition

So, given life in the twenty-first century, where does this leave the human person and his or her relationship with God? How does the Incarnation continue? Where is it evident? Here I want to examine how we see humanity, to explore the worth and dignity of the human person, to focus on the meaning of 'neighbour' and to consider ways in which we might reconfigure society in the light of the current economic crisis. It is my conjecture that valuable lessons can be derived from the body of thinking called Catholic Social Teaching. I am going to explore this, with reference on the way to the philosophy of the ancient Greeks, Rousseau and Hegel, the Enlightenment, the collapse of Communism, the Gospels, the Second Vatican Council and the writings of Popes John Paul II and Benedict XVI.

But first I would like to identify key themes of the current human condition. Contemporary society offers enormous challenges but evidence of great advances in the world too. These, I would say, are the greatest challenges:

- That we are dogged by environmental problems which cause us great foreboding.
- There are huge inequalities in wealth between the developed world and the developing world.
- The developed world faces deep economic woes.
- There is a crisis for children – a crisis of malnutrition in the developing world, and a crisis of dysfunctional families in the affluent West.

But at the same time, we have seen:

- An increasing awareness of our planet, appreciation of it, and desire to combat its troubles.
- Remarkable altruism that has often manifested itself in generous responses to those suffering natural disasters.
- Greater numbers of women being educated.
- Medical progress.

In this context, a combination of strife and success, what is the response of humanity to God and of people to their fellow human beings?

I would like at this juncture to consider one of the most loved parables of Jesus, that of the Good Samaritan. Even though it appears in only one of the Gospels, Luke, it is one of the most familiar. Jesus narrates a tale that begins on the road between Jerusalem and Jericho, where a Jewish man was mugged and left for dead. A priest came by and then a Levite, and both avoided the robbed and injured man and did nothing to help. Then came the Samaritan, whose people and the Jews usually despised one another. But he was moved to pity by the man lying in the dust, helped him with first aid and then paid for him to be looked after at a nearby inn (Luke 10.30–5).

There have been various interpretations of the parable. Augustine suggested that the Samaritan represents Christ saving the sinful soul. Mrs Thatcher thought it was all about proving you can't help people unless you have the financial means to do so. Contemporary interpretations have focused on the query that the original questioner of Jesus asked, 'Who is my neighbour?', and have seen in the parable the point that Christianity must have no truck with ethnic, religious or sectarian prejudice.

But alongside the question 'Who is my neighbour?' is a parallel question we must ask ourselves: 'What does it take for me to be a neighbour?' 'Am I looking at the other with the eye of a neighbour?' The parable of the Good Samaritan makes it clear that this concern for the other is not restricted to those dearest to us but embraces even the stranger. Moving away from focusing on asking 'Who is my neighbour' emphasizes that this parable is not about a defined category but a way of behaving, an attitude.

It means that instead of looking at a person and thinking 'One of us?', you question your own motive and say 'What am I?' It sounds deceptively simple but is constantly challenging; it is what Pope Benedict in his 2011 book *Jesus of Nazareth, Part 2*, called 'the risk of goodness' (Benedict XVI, 2011, p. 199).

Pope Benedict's first encyclical, or teaching document, *Deus Caritas Est*, encapsulated this when he wrote: 'Charity is not a kind of welfare activity which could equally be left to others, but is a part of the Church's nature, an indispensable expression of her very being' (Benedict XVI, 2005, para. 25a). Embracing this concept of charity means looking beyond the confines of our own self-interest. Instead, the *raison d'être* of each believer and the *raison d'être* of the Church as well, are to be a Christian community stretching out towards others. The divine–human exchange that is at the heart of the relationship between God and the human person also requires human-to-human exchange to thrive.

This human-to-human exchange takes more than one form, however. It is much more than the relatively small world of our own self and family and friends but a recognition of the worth and dignity of others. This shapes the way in which we deal with those with whom we come into contact. And while it is not practical or possible to respond to every single person on the planet, it does nevertheless influence the way we see the world. It is Christianity, then, rather than Communism – an ideology exposed as profoundly flawed – that flies the flag for equality.

Yet, Christianity's challenge to believers to recognize the worth and dignity of fellow men and women has not always lifted the veil from their eyes. No doubt when they heard the words of Matthew's Gospel – 'Lord, when were you hungry or thirsty' (Matt. 25.37) – American slave-owners, with great sincerity, considered how they treated their wives and children and thought of themselves as pillars of the community. Yet, they simultaneously viewed other human beings as beneath them, to be left without freedom or dignity. It is a salient lesson to us to consider how future generations might look back and wonder how we could have a taken a particular view of, say, Muslims or Polish migrant workers; of those with a disability; of the baby aborted for having a cleft palate. The slope to what can be defined as almost a de-recognition of our fellow human beings can be a slippery one, full of good intentions. When, for instance, doctors looked after a young man in a coma who had been badly injured after the Hillsborough football disaster, one of them told the High Court that the Liverpool fan's life should come to an end, because he wasn't a person any more.

Contemporary society's focus on individualism recognizes that every person has a value – but in a capitalist society which places so much store by celebrity and wealth, that value is measured in terms of beauty, money and talent, rather than community, neighbourhood or family. Christianity sees the human person as someone defined in terms of relations with others. That young man lying in a coma has a fragile relationship with others but he is still loved by parents, by relations and friends – he is a person in that sense. And if we acknowledge the love of God, then even someone who is friendless and orphaned remains as a person through the love of the Lord. He is essentially valued for himself.

Catholic Teachings for the Contemporary World

I would like here to move from the relationship that we have with those immediately close to us, and those wider relationships with those with whom we come into contact, to a wider perspective: to how we see human persons beyond our immediate ken. One of the curiosities of the contemporary human condition is that just as individualism has strengthened its hold on us, with an emphasis, as I have previously mentioned, on success, fame, money and beauty of the individual – especially with those having, as one TV programme would have it, the X factor – so the world has become interconnected. Radio, television, Twitter, Facebook, rolling news – we have a powerful link with the rest of the globe through advances in technology and communications.

That shrinking of the world stepped up apace after the end of the Second World War and was articulated in the Second Vatican

Council document *Gaudium et Spes* – Joy and Hope. The fathers of the Church who attended the Council were conscious of the great changes that were happening at the start of the Sixties, changes that would inevitably impact on the Christian Churches and the faithful. Thirty years before the term globalization became used, the Vatican Council identified it as a defining feature of the modern age, although its optimism in saying that 'the whole human family is moving gradually together and everywhere is more conscious already of its oneness', seems particularly idealistic today, given the political and economic divisions that separate us.

And yet ... the goal of a universal brotherhood, as articulated in *Gaudium et Spes*, is both at the heart of Christianity and evident in the structure of society. There are undoubtedly close bonds of mutual dependence, from men and women working to meet the needs of their families to the interaction of people in the working world.

The mutual dependence of mankind – the belief that we are intrinsically social beings – led the German philosopher Hegel to assert that an account of the human person must begin not with Rousseau's noble savage – the idea that our existence has its roots in a sort of pre-social animal – but in marriage and the family. From there society develops, through economic community and civil society to the political community and the state. Hegel saw the goal that should be achieved as the might of the State. The Vatican Council's *Gaudium et Spes* went beyond that with its focus on fraternity, the ideal articulated by the German poet Schiller in his Ode to Joy ('All Men Shall Be Brothers'), set to music by Beethoven in his ninth symphony.

This is not a mere phrase expressing idealism, or revolution. It is a succinct summing up of the theology running through the body of thought called Catholic Social Teaching. This teaching provides a powerful means of putting into practice the tenets of Christianity. The idea of autonomous individuals, still shaped by the philosophy of the Enlightenment, is a thin notion of the human person. Catholic Social Teaching is much more optimistic, seeing a person as not merely an economic animal but a social one. It is also focused on the potential of all people, for at Catholic Social

Teaching's heart is the Common Good – the well-being of human persons.

As the fallout of the economic crisis, which has taken its toll on jobs and on families, continues, even deeper issues have come to the surface. The assumption that the economy could provide beneficial outcomes; the confidence we had in democratic government to ensure a society that functions well: these have been fractured by such seismic change. But the crisis has also led to greater questioning of the way in which society functions – and a growing sense that an economic system that was careless of people needs rebuilding with ethical foundations. The idea that religion can in some way play a part in political or economic debate is anathema to many people, who fear that such intervention would lead to theocracy or an even more divided society. I am certainly not suggesting special privileges for religion; rather, that decisions about right action benefit from reason, but religion can also shed light upon the discovery of moral principles. It can help us develop our understanding of the human person and perhaps rediscover or reconfirm principles that we lost in the rush to greed of the past 20 or so years.

This leaves us with challenges: we need to question not only the mistakes and flaws found in the regulation of financial institutions in recent years but the ethics – or lack of them – in our economic system. Are its destructive tendencies the result of allowing the economy to become essentially an autonomous and amoral domain, outside the arena of ordinary moral judgement? Have we let it function, regardless of whom it hurts? Has economic life, in other words, become too important to be left to economists?

In recent years, efforts have been made to ensure that the State increasingly regulates the financial system. But if we assume that this is the only constraint needed on the pursuit of profit, then we are digging ourselves deeper into an amoral hole. While the laws of financial regulation are certainly useful, they cannot supply the principles of right moral behaviour for the common good, in the marketplace or elsewhere. Instead, in a healthy society we need boundaries which derive from the prevailing personal and collective ethics and ethos, present in the culture.

But it is the very ethos of our current society, built on post-Enlightenment secular individualism, that has been our problem. It is this that allowed the aggressive market capitalism which so let us down to flourish. So if we consider how we can reform the kind of economy that we have let be rampant but we don't think again about the culture that allowed it to thrive, then nothing will change. That is why the economic system needs scrutiny according to ethical criteria that are not of its own making. If these criteria are to convince people working and benefitting from the economic system, then they need to be rational, coherent and based on an understanding of mankind, its motivations, talents and flaws. That has always been the business of Christianity.

After the fall of the Communist powers in 1989, many may have thought that not only was this a triumph of freedom, but also a triumph of capitalism – that it was the antithesis of a system which had led to the degradation of human freedom. But within capitalism as practised for the past 20 or so years was not so much a guarantee of freedom but the potential to limit it. The gulag archipelago of the West was not a place of punishment for those with ideas threatening to the system, but a place of despair for those who fell victim to debt, to joblessness, and who were crushed in the rush to greed. Karol Woytyla, later Pope John Paul II, was one of the fiercest critics of Communism, and in his 1960 work *Love and Responsibility* he argued that the great moral imperative is for us to avoid using others – and that is the ethical basis of freedom. That moral imperative allows us to interact without reducing others to objects by manipulating them. But consider how rampant capitalism has allowed some to trample over others.

'The evil of our time', Woytyla wrote in a letter to the French theologian Henri de Lubac, 'consists in the first place in a kind of degradation, indeed in a pulverization of the fundamental uniqueness of each human person' (cited by de Lubac, 1989, pp. 171–2). That degradation of the human person can be caused by both the collectivism of the old communist order but also by the individualism and greed of what was thought the only alternative – the capitalism of the West. As the Jesuit theologian James Hanvey has put it, 'The market is a brutal and morally unaccountable instrument, not essentially concerned with people except in so far as they are of use' (Caritas Social Action Network, 2011, p. 24).

Twin Pillars of Catholic Social Teaching

So what can there be in its place? Is there a way of enhancing the way we form society so that each human person is accorded respect and dignity; so that society functions well as a community of mutually dependent and valued persons. In other words is there a way in which God is incarnated in our relations with others? Catholic Social Teaching provides guiding principles based on reflection on human history and nature, in the light of the gospel. Its criteria are not unique to Catholics; indeed its roots lie in philosophy that predates Christianity and whose influence continues to be felt in modern Western culture – something which indicates that not only people of faith but all those concerned with ethics can understand and implement them. Its logical coherence and firm foundation on clearly stated moral and philosophical principles can make it an effective tool for analysis of recent events. And rarely has there been a more urgent case for a global economy that serves human flourishing rather than human greed. Catholic Social Teaching makes the case for policies and practices that above all respect the dignity and worth of each person. Rather than perceive a person as an isolated individual, Catholic Social Teaching sees him or her as a social being, especially those most affected by the turbulence of recent years: the poor, children in difficult family situations.

What keeps the focus on the most vulnerable in society – the same people of whom we hear so much in the Gospels and whom we are urged to empower – are two specific principles in Catholic Social Teaching: solidarity and subsidiarity. Today these two words have rather particular associations for many people: Solidarity probably signifies to most people a Polish trade union, while subsidiarity conjures up ideas of EU jargon. But both usages have their roots in Catholic Social Teaching.

Solidarity has a rich tradition in Catholic Social Teaching and is considered both as a principle by which right moral actions can be judged and as a virtue to be cultivated in individuals, communities and society. It expresses our relatedness as children of God – a relatedness that means we have obligations to one another. In a society of such obligations, exploitation and oppression of one another's fellow human beings cannot be countenanced. Instead, people must stand together in the face of hardships. This focus on the collaboration of people is not, however, an acceptance of collectivism. Rather it is an acknowledgement of both the need for us to work together for the betterment of society and the need to leave space for individual freedom. This is the corrective – the perception that we are both free individuals and social beings – that is needed to counter the isolationism and individualism of recent years in the West. James Hanvey puts it powerfully. Solidarity, he says, 'requires that we think not only in terms of "me" but also in terms of "we". It not only recognises the social and interpersonal reality of the human person, it goes beyond a utilitarian interdependency to the expression of a profound moral vision ... It requires more than a simple intellectual or social assent but a moral conversion. It is the commitment to the good of all, not just a personal group, or national good.' And if solidarity is to be real, says Hanvey, 'it requires us to address those issues which generate and sustain injustice and unjust inequalities' (Caritas Social Action Network, p. 24).

The other twin pillar of Catholic Social Teaching, subsidiarity, is a principle that proposes that decisions and functions should be carried out as closely as possible to the people they affect. In other words, the State must help groups and organizations to thrive to contribute to the Common Good but it should not interfere in what they do. In the European Union, this principle has come to mean the rights of sovereign states to determine their own social policy, moving in the hands of some to an almost neoliberal rejection of the social market. But in a different sphere the idea of subsidiarity is gaining credence, via Red Toryism, the thinking of Phillip Blond which inspired David Cameron's early flagship policy the Big Society. This includes a growing interest in localism, and the enabling of people in their communities to work together for the Common Good without constant reference to the State. Of course we know that there are many instances of generosity at the local level, particularly in the voluntary sector. And yet we can all see evidence around us too of a decline in the spirit of solidarity and subsidiarity, with many people far more isolated than ever, and living alone. There is also a lingering assumption by some that the State will best be left to run things. The networks between people, often called social capital, have declined in many areas. If it is to be replenished, then we will have to rediscover our own personal responsibility, our mutual dependence and a sense of service.

Given the extent to which subsidiarity chimes with certain politicians, there is some suspicion that it is a theory of privatization. It most definitely does not mean that. Its origins are the Latin word, *subsidium*, which means help or assistance. It involves the recognition on the part of a higher authority that there is another form of power at a lower level and that this lower level encourages human flourishing. The higher authority in turn, according to the theory of subsidiarity, helps the lower level to benefit society.

In a recent encyclical, *Caritas in Veritate*, Pope Benedict addressed in detail the economic times in which we live. He articulated a challenge to those who believe there is nothing to be done about the way in which some succeed while others flounder. 'It is erroneous', he said, 'to hold that the market economy has an inbuilt need for a quota of poverty and underdevelopment in order to function at its best. It is in the interests of the market to promote emancipation' (Benedict XVI, 2009, para. 35).

A well-functioning market, if it is to promote emancipation, needs a legal structure; it needs to provide essential goods and services, it needs a collective agreed morality of individuals and a vital civic society. And if that market is to benefit all of society, all human persons, then it needs to focus on more than profit and growth. It needs a business ethic. The Christian perspective of the human person can contribute here, I believe, because it reminds us that the human person should be the focus of the business ethic, rather than profit, whatever the cost.

Wealth creation is of course of benefit to us, but to paraphrase scripture, wealth creation was made for man; man was not made for wealth creation.

What we do with that wealth creation depends on persons, and that means it depends on personality. Regulation will not make the markets improve our society to be a place of fellowship and human flourishing, just as league tables will not make a school anything more than an exam factory. But a focus on the person and on personality will help. So, how to do this? One way is to dust off the language of virtue. Virtue recognizes that we are moral creatures, that we do what is right for no reason other than it is right. The point isn't a possible reward or a legal obligation, or yet more regulations. If we focus on virtue, on being prudent, on being courageous, on being just, or modest, or temperate – both as individuals and as a society – then there is a shift in thinking away from 'What do I get out of this?', or 'Who are you? Who do you think you are?' to the question I posed in relation to the parable of the Good Samaritan: 'What does it take for me to be a neighbour?'

Pope Benedict has called for ways of 'civilizing the economy', meaning both humanizing the market and opening it to the pursuit of social ends. In *Caritas in Veritate* he notes that 'Catholic Social Teaching holds that authentically human social relationships of friendship, solidarity and reciprocity can also be conducted within economic activity, and not only outside it or 'after' it.' He goes on to describe the 'great challenge before us' as one of demonstrating that 'in commercial relationships the principle of gratuitousness and the logic of gift as an expression of fraternity can and must find their place within normal economic activity' (Benedict XVI, 2009, para. 36).

This idea of gratuitousness and of gift is often a baffling one for English speakers. They are concepts that don't quite add up, when we're used to a gift being something you receive on a birthday, and something gratuitous usually being an insult. Sometimes gratuitousness can be translated as indebtedness, but that too is awkward, suggesting something owed. The principle of gratuity means that we live and flourish from resources that we alone cannot create or sustain. In a world dominated by the belief that everything and everybody has a price, this is profoundly challenging. But what is freely given – goodness – communicates itself, and the goodness of humanity, by way of the classical virtues, will enhance not only our personal relationships but also civic and public life.

Conclusion

The importance of how we act, not only as individuals, but also as part of wider society, was evident not only in the economic crisis but also in the upheavals of the riots of summer 2011. The turmoil of our city streets highlighted how easily reason can be put to one side, and how quickly there can be a breakdown of public order. Yet, in their reaction to the riots, many people not only expressed outrage about this anarchy but a desire to come together collectively to clean up and to mourn those who had died. In other words, it was a moment to express solidarity. That was encouraging, but the 'thinness' of contemporary society was evident – the collective beliefs, the collective values, the collective morality is waning. Yet there is a sense too that amid the dissatisfaction, there is the possibility of a reassessment of values, a questioning of the world we have made for ourselves, and the chance of something else.

Human beings are constantly developing or becoming. Christianity sees the human person as not bound by the material or historical world but as a creature liberated to look beyond it. He or she has a relationship not only with others immediately around them but a connection with others and with God, evidenced by their questioning, by their potential and their yearning for something beyond them. A person is not just what he or she does, or how he or she acts. Think of the traditional question asked of a stranger at a party: 'What do you do?', making the person who isn't working feel inadequate. As Rowan Williams has said, what makes the human person human is independent of someone else's judgement of failure or success, profit or loss (p. 10). What makes humanity human is what is given unconditionally: and in Christian terms, that is love, which is rooted in God.

Bibliography

Documents

Pope Benedict XVI, 2005, *Deus Caritas Est*, Rome: The Holy See.
Pope Benedict XVI, 2009, *Caritas in Veritate*, Rome: The Holy See.
Bishops' Conference of England and Wales, 2010, *Choosing the Common Good*, Stoke-on-Trent: Alive Publishing.
Brakkenstein Community of Blessed Sacrament Fathers, 1973, *Rule for a New Brother, Holland*, London: Darton Longman and Todd.
Caritas Social Action Network, 2011, *A Common Endeavour*, report of a conference held at Liverpool Hope University, Liverpool, February 2011.
Second Vatican Council, 1965(a), *Gaudium et Spes* (Pastoral constitution on the Church in the modern world), Rome: The Holy See, online, available at: www.vatican.va (accessed 10 January 2013).
Second Vatican Council, 1965(b), *Nostra Aetate* (Declaration on the relation of the Church to non-Christian religions), Rome: The Holy See, online, available at: www.vatican.va (accessed 10 January 2013).

Books and articles

Matthew Arnold, 1852, 'The Buried Life', *Poetry Foundation*, online, available at: http://www.poetryfoundation.org/poem/172841 (accessed 10 January 2013).
Nicholas Boyle, 2005, 'On Earth, as it is in Heaven', *The Tablet*, 9 July, London: The Tablet Publishing Company.
Ed Cassidy and G. Eoin, 2009, *Who is My Neighbour?* Dublin: Veritas.
Henri de Lubac, 1989, *At the Service of the Church: Henri de Lubac Reflects on the Circumstances that Occasioned His Writings*, San Francisco: Ignatius Press.
Daniel McDonald (ed.), 2010, *Catholic Social Teaching in Global Perspective*, Maryknoll NY: Orbis Books.
Daniel O'Leary, 2011, *Unmasking God*, Dublin: Columba.
Joseph Ratzinger/Pope Benedict XVI, 2011, *Jesus of Nazareth, Part 2: Holy Week, from the Entrance into Jerusalem to the Resurrection*, London: Catholic Truth Society.
George Weigel, 2001, *Witness to Hope*, London: Harper Collins.
Rowan Williams and Larry Elliott, 2010, *Crisis and Recovery – Ethics, Economics and Justice*, London: Macmillan.
Karol Woytyla/Pope John Paul II, rev. 1993, *Love and Responsibility*, San Francisco: Ignatius Press.

8

Church and Politics: 'My Kingdom is not of this World' Really?

JAMES JONES

I remember as a young school teacher, heavily involved in community work and actively engaged in setting up the first Volunteer Bureau which brought me into contact with the legendary radical figure the Revd Nicolas Stacey, who by then had given up his priestly duties and become Director of Social Services for Kent, being approached by a political grandee to find out whether I would like to stand for the Local Council. It was not a foreign idea; my political hero since student days was William Wilberforce. I was possessed of that youthful zeal to change the world which, I hope is still evident, has not entirely left me! However, as I contemplated the possibilities and my own abilities, two distinct paths lay ahead: one the Church, the other politics. I eventually chose the Church (or as I would prefer to say God called me to the Church) because although I am keenly interested in politics – its personalities as well as it philosophies – I continue to hold the view that in the realm of changing people's hearts and minds you have to first change people's hearts before you can change their minds.

Although some of the great political campaigners and orators have, like preachers, sought first to change hearts, political discourse today is principally focused on argumentation and advertising, winning the argument in the TV debate is the goal. I recall sitting next to a leading Trade Union official in a football stadium at a Billy Graham rally during Mission England.

As hundreds of people poured on to the pitch in response to his appeal to follow Christ, he turned to me and whispered wistfully, 'this is what the Trade Union movement used to be like'. The Church, as I saw it as a young man, was about converting the soul, changing the heart and winning the person for Christ. How could a politician appeal successfully to the electorate for a more just and compassionate, less selfish and materialistic society, if the hearts of the people were not already turned in this direction? To that end the Church seemed to have a prior claim on me and my particular gifts. It is where I still stand, in that I believe that the spiritual renewal of our people is a prerequisite in creating a just society that is more at peace with itself.

Using Religion to Change People's Hearts

We cannot pretend that the Church as an institution does not face some enormous challenges at present, such as the internal controversies over women bishops and sexual ethics, which impede its engagement with the world. Yet at its most essential the Christian religion is about a relationship with God: 'He converteth my soul' as the Book of Common Prayer beautifully expresses Psalm 23, and to such an extent that we are led in the words of the prophet Micah to walk humbly with God, to act justly and to love mercy. This is the social impact of spiritual renewal. It should make one hunger for justice.

Church and politics are not two parallel lines; rather they are two live wires, side by side, which when they touch should ignite and explode. They do when someone from one discipline dares to comment on the other. I experienced this in a consultation with Oliver Letwin, Director of Policy for the Conservative Party, who spoke of the opprobrium heaped upon him for daring to speak of the Politics of Beauty or the Politics of Love. The same antagonism is visited upon church leaders who venture into the political sphere. The frequent retort from politicians to church leaders, especially if they do not like the hue of their hectoring, is to quote Jesus: 'My Kingdom is not of this world.' This, they think, is the knock-down argument to silence them, Jesus saying that the Christian faith has nothing to do with the real world of politics. Not only is it impossible to square this with the teaching and activity of Jesus as set out in the Nazareth Manifesto in Luke 4, about healing the sick and liberating the oppressed, these rendered words of Jesus misrepresent what he actually said. The original Greek text records Jesus saying something very different: 'My Kingdom is not *from* this world.' In other words, faced with the power and authority of Pontius Pilate, Jesus was telling him and the world that his own authority to rule, indeed all his inner resource, came from God.

Everything Jesus did and taught was about extending the rule of God on earth. It is explicitly present in the Lord's Prayer where Jesus calls us to pray for the coming of God's Kingdom and the doing of God's will on earth as it is done in heaven. The radical nature of this prayer and its political ramifications were expounded by Charles Elliot in his classic *Praying the Kingdom*. The great twentieth-century apologist, Lesslie Newbigin, in that other classic *The Other Side of 1984*, answered the protest against the Church engaging in politics by writing 'What right have we got to withdraw from the Sovereignty of God any aspect of his kingdom?' (Newbiggin, 1990).

It was Stephen Green's book *Good Value* that opened my eyes to another dimension of God's Kingdom. Stephen Green is a former chairman of HSBC and a priest in the Church of England, and reflects in his book on the banking crisis. He writes about globalization which he sees not as an 'ism' as in Capitalism or Communism but as a phenomenon, inevitable to human progress (Green, 2010). It struck me that although the word globalization is recently coined, the concept is something that Jesus talked and taught about more than any other subject. Of course, he did not use the word 'globalization'. Rather, he talked about 'kingdom', the steady expansive extension of God's rule over the earth and the climactic establishing of the values of his kingdom. Christians ought to be cautious when we criticize globalization as a phenomenon. We have been at it longer than Starbucks or McDonald's! If there are any questions to be raised about globalization it is not about the phenomenon itself but about the values of some of the globalizing empires.

Although religion is about changing people's hearts it is also about discerning worth and value. If changing hearts constitutes the ploughing of fields, then values are the seeds to be sown. This in turn yields the crop that political husbandry harvests for the common good. It is to values in six different areas that I wish to turn my attention in this chapter. Freedom, Fairness, Family, Friendship, Faith and the Future. Each of these subjects merits its own chapter, and the purpose is not to give an exhaustive critique of each but to show in each of these six areas how certain values, what Christians sometimes call Kingdom Values, might impact on public policy. This offering is predicated on the biblical principle expressed in Romans 12—13 that those elected and appointed to Government are so by divine permission and are, whether or not they recognize the description, 'Deacons of God' (Rom. 13.4).

It is remarkable that St Paul, who both claimed the privileges of the Roman State by insisting '*Civis Romanus sum*' ('I am a Roman Citizen') and fell victim to its judgement, ascribes this high calling to the officials of the Roman Empire at a time when Nero was emperor. This informs my own understanding of the State which although imperfect is ordained by God for the common good and, however flawed, is preferable to anarchy. Of course, there will be times when people of Christian faith will take issue with how the State acts but even if they are moved to civil disobedience they accept the State's authority to move against them. This happened in the New Testament church when the disciples were persecuted and denied their freedom to preach the Resurrection. Peter summarized their predicament 'Whether it is right in God's sight to listen to you rather than to God, you must judge; for we cannot keep from speaking about what we have seen and heard.' They reserved the right to challenge the State and took the consequences, accepting the authority of the State to punish them even though it was in the wrong. It is not a perfect parallel but it is similar to a game of football, in which the players and spectators ultimately have to accept the decisions of the referee even when they passionately believe them to be wrong.

Freedom

The New Testament church began its life in an occupied land under the rule of the Roman Empire. It lived in the cauldron of a clash of cultures. There was tension between the Jewish religious authorities and the provincial leadership of Rome. This came to a head over the arrest, trial and execution of Jesus. After the death and resurrection of Jesus, and the rapid increase in the number of disciples, this new and burgeoning sect came to the point of being proscribed by both the Jewish religious authorities and Rome itself. Hauled before the religious Council they were told 'not to speak at all in the name of Jesus'.

The response of Peter and the disciples was to face the intimidation and to preach 'the word of God with boldness' (Acts 4.31 ESV). The word 'boldness' in its different forms occurs nine times in Acts. The word in Greek is *parresia*. It is from classical Greek meaning 'freedom of speech'. In other words, the early Christians in the face of bitter persecution seemed to claim a God-given right to freedom of expression. Two thousand years of Christian history has borne witness to how their right to freedom of speech borrowed from the Graeco-Roman world has been claimed by Christians at great personal cost and the shedding of much martyrs' blood. This witness to freedom has informed Western civilization and ensured that it is one of the most enduring features of our own culture.

The degree to which we can allow such freedom has become a subject of political debate. Clearly every society has to strike a balance between personal liberty and national security. It is like holding a spirit-level and ensuring the air bubble rests in the middle. But there are reactionary forces at work which would force us to move away from that cherished personal freedom. I am increasingly uncomfortable with the legislation that inhibits freedom of speech through the Incitement to Religious Hatred Act. I fully support the intention, to protect good relationships between faith communities, but I am deeply worried by the unintended consequences which I fear do the opposite. Such a law provides a field day when zealous converts to one faith encounter zealous believers of another and are reported to equally zealous police officers trying to make a name for themselves on the equality and diversity agenda. I fear that recent cases such as the 2009 dispute in Liverpool over criticism of the complainant's hijab, if repeated, could undermine the excellent relationships that have been built up between Christian and Muslim communities.

There is another reason to question this well-meaning but badly conceived legislation. As a pastor I am very aware of the power that religious leaders have over their followers and the tragic history of abuse especially of children and women. I do not think that such leaders of religions should be protected from criticism, ridicule or satire. I know what it is like to be misrepresented in and by the media, but I would rather live with that difficulty and know that the weak and vulnerable are protected from abusive religion through a free press and a culture of responsible freedom.

This episode in the Acts of the Apostles has for me another important dimension. The freedom to express yourself lies at the heart of a truly free society. I think there is an inextricable link between freedom of expression and economic freedom. The moment any society controls completely the means of production and distribution, it is in control of what can be expressed and communicated. But at its most basic a belief in the freedom of expression requires a person, should they so wish, to be free to be able to save and buy a printer and distribute their ideas. On the spectrum with laissez-faire capitalism at one end and totalitarianism at the other there is a strong Christian pressure in the name of freedom pulling away from totalitarianism, but not so far as to push completely in the direction of laissez-faire capitalism, because the next important principle that a Christian longs to see incorporated into our common life is that of fairness and justice.

Fairness

Justice is a constant theme throughout the scriptures. The Prophets of the Old Testament hammered home the message that God expected his people to act justly and to love mercy. In particular, they were to address the needs of widows, orphans and strangers. In a society where welfare was centred on the family (children were your old-age pension and medical insurance wrapped up in one, which is why there may have been so few incidents of child abuse), widows, orphans and strangers were the socially excluded, the marginalized, and those on the edge of opportunity. Lacking equality of opportunity to flourish, it was the responsibility of the wider community to ensure their protection and prosperity. It is in this biblical example that we find a political model of addressing inequality. Whatever the merits and pitfalls of capitalism and the market (the recent economic crisis struck me as a vindication of the market that did in effect blow the whistle on fantasy borrowing, excessive risk-taking and inflated loans), they have to be tempered by other principles that protect the weak and include those marginalized through no fault of their own.

I served on the Debt Commission under Lord Griffiths. In Hull and Liverpool I have been involved in different government schemes to deal with deprivation and to regenerate our cities – the Single Regeneration Bids and the New Deal for Communities. I chaired the New Deal Board in Liverpool for four years, and have been instrumental in building three City Academies in areas of poverty in partnership with the Catholic Archdiocese. These interventions have targeted what I call areas of 'consolidated poverty', which is not just economic poverty but vandalized public space, emotional deprivation through inadequate parenting, generational unemployment and low educational achievement and aspiration. Being born into a culture of consolidated poverty plunges a child into an inequality that is difficult for them to escape.

My own involvement has led me to conclude that any regeneration strategy has to be a combination of the spiritual, economic and social that targets low self-esteem, creates real jobs and local wealth and involves and enables local people to shape their own future. Consolidated poverty is multi-dimensional and calls for an integrated strategy. Sadly, too much of the external funding given to regeneration programmes has been showered on the areas instead of being channelled to irrigate them. Many of our cities, especially in the north of England, are in danger of suffering from urban diabetes. This is where the blood pumps around the heart of the city in prestigious projects such as concert halls and galleries but fails to circulate around the whole body so that the outer estates at the extremities, which the wealth fails to reach, end up atrophying and dying. The gospel image that has touched me both in Hull and Liverpool is the figure of Jesus standing outside the city and weeping, pleading: 'If only you know the things that make for peace.' Richard Wilkinson in his book *The Spirit Level* shows by comparison with other countries that where there is less of a gap between rich and poor, where the equality of opportunity is greater, then there is greater social stability and less dysfunctional behaviour, and more to the point, fewer people in prison. Although comparing one nation with another is not an exact science, even Wilkinson's critics admit that 'the general tendency of extreme inequality is to make people fear and mistrust one another more' (Moore, 2010). Christians called by Jesus to seek his Kingdom and his justice will want interventions to moderate market forces and strategies from Government to ensure greater opportunities especially for disadvantaged children and young people.

Family

The most serious disadvantage inflicted upon children is the emotional deprivation that flows from inadequate or absentee parenting. A recent media report highlighted the trial of two young brothers in Edlington who abducted and nearly killed two other children. As is so frequently the case, the cruelty and emotional numbness of the perpetrators can be traced back to neglect by their parents. I welcome the political debate about the family that has been triggered by Prime Minister David Cameron's intention to support marriage in the tax and benefit system. Some of us have been calling for this for a long time. I was making the call for it 12 years ago when I was Bishop of Hull and calling for transferrable tax allowances for married couples with children and a single income. Those opposed protest that you shouldn't have to bribe people to get married. These and other objections miss the most salient point. It is surely a matter of justice that a household of two with two incomes should be taxed differently from a household of three, four or five where there is only one income because the parents have decided to give priority to the nurture of the child by (a) committing themselves to each other and (b) one of them dedicating themselves to the development of the children.

We need a renewed political sense of the importance of the family. As Bishop for Prisons I meet with and listen to many prisoners. Time and again their anomic stories begin with parental neglect. This is not offenders seeking to shift the blame. It is simply a common narrative that adult dysfunctional behaviour often begins with a child's being treated dysfunctionally. The present Conservative–Liberal Democrat coalition Government has channelled billions of pounds into supporting children, but they and previous administrations have failed to ensure the most fundamental support, which is to strengthen the God-given unit designed to bring a child to emotional, social, intellectual and moral maturity. As all pastors know, we live not in an ideal world but in one that is full of casualties of the Fall. Society must make provision for those who fail along the way but not at the expense of reinforcing the one institution that has a proven track record in delivering more emotionally, socially, intellectually and morally adjusted young people. In its most recent report, CARE has shown that the chances of a child living in a single-parent household by the age of five are one in two if they begin life with a cohabiting couple and one in 12 with a married couple.

As well as reinforcing the social value of marriage and the family I believe the Government ought also to support all parents regardless of marital status in the heavy responsibility of child development. The present Government has added to an excellent network of Children Centres and Sure Start programmes. The problem is that they are failing to reach some of the neediest families. We need new strategies to engage the hard-to-reach parents who are the ones most at risk of neglecting their children and abandoning them to dysfunctionality and criminal behaviour. We need to learn from countries such as Austria, Hungary, France and Mexico where payments called 'conditional cash transfers' have successfully drawn hard-to-reach parents into more effective parenting and parenting programmes. I believe the Church should speak prophetically from the scriptures to those aspiring to govern us that marriage and the family form a fundamental institution which we neglect at our peril and risk the future stability of society.

Friendship

We are all aware of the changing social landscape to which, of course, both emigration and immigration contribute significantly. No student of British history can deny that these isles have been shaped by waves of population movement. It is difficult to pinpoint any decade in the past one thousand years and say that 'this' was the definitive era where no change took place. Yet even though we recognize that culture evolves, we also know that social stability depends on the graduation of such cultural evolution. Decisions about the numbers of immigrants and asylum seekers to be admitted require political wisdom, judgement and courage and depend upon the impact these admissions will have on services and the rapidity of social change. Religious leaders do not envy our political counterparts their onerous responsibilities, but at the same time, speaking up as advocates of 'the stranger' in the tradition of the biblical prophets, we make a passionate plea for friendship with those who migrate to these shores.

The city of Liverpool is home to the oldest Islamic Prayer Room in the UK. It is being converted into a Heritage and Education Centre for British Islam. There is nothing exceptional in that, except that the leaders of the Muslim community invited me, a Christian, to be the Patron. I accepted because although I believe there are some fundamental differences between our two faiths and although I believe that Christianity is formative of our culture, I also believe that this is a way of my obeying the second great Commandment to love my neighbour as myself. Furthermore, I believe that the future stability of our society and the world depends on good relationships between the faith communities. I am under no illusion about some of the sinister forces seeking succour and support in Islam, but I also believe that at the same time as resisting these vigorously we should also encourage the best examples of British Islam to integrate into our society.

One episode in particular from the Gospels has been formative in my own attitude to relationships with other ethnic groups. The Cleansing of the Temple is seen as a statement against commercialism but that is only half the story, if that. Jesus quotes from Isaiah and Jeremiah, 'My house shall be a house of prayer for all peoples.' He's giving a vision of the Temple as a place where people of different ethnicities are all welcome. The quote is all the more significant when you realize that he overturned the merchants' tables in the Temple Court which had been set aside for the other races to draw near to God – the Court of the Gentiles. What made him angry was that the Gentiles, the other races, had been denied their sacred space, which Jesus promptly restored to them by refusing to let anyone else move around in it. It is that degree of hospitality that should mark our welcome of other ethnic groups. I long for the day when the Church of England itself might embrace and reflect that hospitality.

Of course, this hand of friendship begs the question about how much integration will impact on the character of the nation and upon the faith and the role of the Established Church. Interestingly, although there are voices calling for disestablishment, these are not coming from minority faiths, who see the Church of England as holding the ground for the importance of faith to our national life, but rather from secularists, who seem to resent the influence of the Church in public life.

Faith

Historically the Christian faith has shaped our culture. If you consider those things that are distinctly English, namely our laws, our liberty, our language, our literature and our learning, they are all marked by the spirit and ethos of Christianity as surely as our landscape is studded with the jewels of our historic churches and cathedrals. This is a heritage worth conserving not just because of its cultural significance but because, and I know I now speak explicitly from the view of faith, we believe that the Christian faith speaks timeless truth to a changing world. The Church of England occupies a unique place historically, culturally and constitutionally. Its extraordinary network of parish churches means that there is not a corner of England, from the deepest rural areas to the innermost city estates via the leafiest suburbs, that is not covered by a caring and praying community. It gives the Church of England and its ministers authority to speak about comfortable and uncomfortable England because quite simply we are there on the ground. Around the country its presence is valued by more than just its members. I think we need to be more robust in defending our faith and in articulating our role more clearly as the convenor of faith communities, as the source of cohesion in many rural and urban areas, as the continuity to civic leadership in towns and cities and as the celebrant of our common life at both a national and local level.

The parish church exists not just for members of the congregation but also for all who live in the parish. It expresses our understanding of God's Kingdom that it is not just the Church but embraces the world. This is why the Church can never be indifferent to politics. Although, as Lesslie Newbigin insisted, we cannot drive a wedge between faith and politics because God is concerned with every aspect of life, it is unwise for the Church to identify itself with and endorse any political party. This time-honoured line was breached recently by the General Synod who for perfectly understandable reasons wanted to express alarm at the rise of the BNP and its racist policies. Unfortunately by proscribing membership of the BNP it inserted the thin edge of the wedge into the separation of faith from party politics. Telling people not to vote for one party is tantamount to telling them to vote for the other. The Church should confine itself to expounding the theological and moral principles upon which public policy should be built. It may even stray into areas of policy. It should not however enter the polling booth by steering its members on how to vote. As to the BNP, the Church must teach the moral repugnance of racism and urge its members to exercise their vote as responsible citizens.

The Future

In conclusion I turn to the future and in particular the future of the planet. Adam Smith, whose *Wealth of Nations* laid the foundations for the Western economy, was in no doubt that the danger that threatened both Government and society was profligacy. He did so at a time when there was no awareness, as there is today, of the threat to the earth's ecological stability. The earth is not a limitless larder.

In a hundred years' time future historians may look back on our era amazed that we could have called ourselves, so comfortably, 'consumers'. Were we not aware of the meaning of the word? Did we not have the science to inform us of the danger done by so much consumption? Laying aside all the debates about the science of climate change, Christians have had a duty as old as the Bible itself to have a God-like dominion over, and an Adam-like service to, the earth (Genesis 1.28 and 2.15). Yet it has taken a long time for Christians, with a few notable exceptions, to grasp the theological and moral imperatives to care for God's creation. This is an example where the Church for all its talk about being prophetic and speaking out about justice has to admit that the prophetic voice on the environment has come from outside the Church. It is not the only one to be so slow. The major political parties have at last come on board, and it is interesting to observe a political party with the title Conservative adopting policies on conserving consonant with its own name!

I have written and lectured elsewhere about the connection between Jesus and the earth, but the one political and fiscal point I would like to emphasize here is that we should use the tax system to express these biblical and ecological values. Green taxes should not be imposed simply as a means of Government raising more revenue for profligate spending. Rather, we should see a shift in favour of encouraging the conservation of natural resources. I anticipate that one day, out of necessity, the Government will abolish income tax and encourage people to enjoy fully the rewards of their labour without penalty; they would then shift the burden of taxation on to resources so that the more you used and consumed the greater tax you would pay. There would need to be a mechanism to protect the poor and vulnerable but this shift would have the effect of making us more responsible and disciplined in our consumption of limited resources which in the next 40 years will need to sustain an extra three billion people on the earth.

As a postscript I will comment on the one area where Church and politics come face to face, where sometimes the two live wires touch and, if not explode, certainly spark: the House of Lords. I believe any proposal to replace an appointed second Chamber with a fully elected House would be a mistake. I fear our electoral system simply would not deliver the set of skills and expertise that are required for a revising Chamber. Here I quote briefly from a speech I made in the House of Lords (July 2009) in a debate on constitutional reform initiated by the Liberal Democrats.

The truth is that in today's world, election, especially in this media-dominated culture in which we live, does not always deliver what is needed. Election delivers up the political class. I respect the political class, and not even in the present climate would I dare to rubbish it. However, it is too narrow a constituency to produce what is needed, especially in this House, for a revising and legislating Assembly. We need to recover the unity of Parliament in the constitutional debate – two Houses but one Parliament: a Commons that is elected and with the authority of having the last word, and a revising Chamber to advise, revise and refine the legislation. Such a revising Chamber should be made up of what is in effect and what could be called the elders of our society: men and women experienced in different walks of life, who, from their expertise and wisdom, can shape the laws that govern our common life. Such people cannot be limited to the political class but must be recruited and appointed with transparency and accountability and for fixed terms.

In this one Parliament, there should be mutuality between the two Houses, each distinctive in character and composition but mutually dependent, the elected looking to the other for wisdom of experience, the appointed deferring to the elected and acknowledging their authority to have the last word as the voice of the people: one Parliament of two Houses under the Crown, as a sign that our own accountability is in two directions: below to the people, above to the source of our moral intuition. I hope that this debate on constitutional renewal will not set the one House against the other. I hope that it will not force one House to imitate or to compete with the other. I hope that we can recognize our distinctiveness and not be afraid of having two Houses of different character within the one Parliament.

The place of the bishops in such a Chamber is as spiritual leaders to sit alongside other elders in our society. Speaking personally I am conscious that although the symbol and ritual of the Crown suggests that our authority to sit there comes from above, it is the authority from below, from being connected with life in the parishes, urban, rural, outer estates and suburban, that enables and equips me and my colleagues to contribute to the debates and the public policy. Since it is a unique Christian insight that the One from above is revealed in the One from below, the Word made flesh, I dare to believe what the bishops draw upon when listening to the people on the ground is in fact the voice of the One from above, whose Kingdom will come one day.

Maranatha. Even so, Lord, come quickly.

Bibliography

Stephen Green, 2010, *Good Value: Choosing a Better Life in Business*, London: Penguin.

Charles Moore, 2010, 'Inequality is not a social illness to be "cured"', *The Daily Telegraph*, 9 February.

Lesslie Newbiggin, 1990, *The Other Side of 1984: Questions for the Churches*, Geneva: World Council of Churches.

Adam Smith, 1982, *The Wealth of Nations*, London: Penguin.

Richard Wilkinson and Kate Pickett, 2010, *The Spirit Level: Why Equality is Better for Everyone*, London: Penguin.

9

The Church, the State and Our Schools: A Relationship that Can Still Work?

ESTELLE MORRIS

The debate about the role of the Church in our education system is not new, but it has certainly taken on a renewed passion and vigour in recent years. The formal education relationship between the Church and the State goes back well over a century, and of course the Church predates the State as a provider of formal education. This is not a marginal debate. There are almost 7000 faith schools in England, just over a third of all schools, educating almost 25 per cent of pupils (DfE, 2012).

The numbers have increased as government has sought to diversify school ethos and ownership. With the emphasis on a new wave of academies and Free Schools, the role of faith schools in the state education system is likely to expand further, with about a third of the Free Schools already open or announced coming into this category. Over the years, the arguments for and against faith schools have barely changed; it is the social, economic and political environment of the times that have propelled the issue into the limelight and given them a new urgency.

The origins of faith schools are twofold. First, the Church sought to provide education for the poor and excluded. Many of the most prestigious independent schools today, such as Winchester, started as schools for poor children. Second, the Church saw as its prime aim the promotion and defence of the faith. The National

Society for the Education of the Poor was founded in 1811 for the 'education of the poor in the principles of the Established Church'. Today we would see these two objectives – educating the poor and promoting the faith – as being unrelated. Centuries ago, they would have been considered one and the same.

The involvement of the Church of England in providing schools strengthened its role in the lives of families, communities and the nation. To this day, most Church of England schools are small rural primary schools at the centre of villages and towns. They were, and in some cases still are, an essential part of the fabric of community life. It is not surprising, therefore, that other religious groups would want to do the same for the communities they served. New immigrant groups, motivated by the same twin ambitions of educating the children of their congregations and protecting and promoting their faith, began to establish their own schools.

There was a rapid increase in the number of Roman Catholic schools between 1847 and 1906, reflecting the religious back-grounds of people newly arrived in the country. The Catholic Poor School Commission became the Catholic Education Service, and new Catholic independent and grammar schools were established. Unlike the Church of England however, the Catholic Church was not the established Church in England, and their schools, in part, offered, 'A cultural and faith bastion against the potentially polluting effect of hegemonic Protestantism and secular rational-ism' (Grace, 2002, p. 8). The Methodist Church responded to the domination of elementary education by the Church of England and Roman Catholic Churches by opening its own schools in the nineteenth century. They were, and still are, mostly situated in the North of England where Methodism was strong. The Manchester Jewish School was established in 1853.

A pattern had been established that has been repeated right through to the twenty-first century. Faith groups have rarely been content with merely providing religious education outside of school but have wanted to be part of the formal system of edu-cation. Many had the added incentive of protecting a minority faith group in a county with an established Church.

The Evolution of Faith-based Education

Before the 1870 Education Act, the State had no direct role. However, faith schools had developed unevenly across the country and the purpose of the 1870 Act was to fill the gap and provide education where it had not been provided by other organizations. The education partnership between Church and State was born. Successive legislation shaped the relationship, and the 1944 Education Act laid down a framework for church schools which still exists today. It established the principle that children could be educated in accordance with their parents' wishes, and developed the framework for Voluntary Aided and Voluntary Controlled schools.

The Act legislated for the role of faith-based schools in the post-war state education system. The Church would continue partly to fund the schools and in return would retain influence and control through its role on the governing bodies. Crucially, it retained the right both to admit pupils and to employ staff based on their religious faith. With the exception of religious education, schools are governed by the education requirements that affect all state schools, including the national curriculum, assessment and accountability frameworks. There has continued to be a strong relationship between the Church and government. Any changes have been evolutionary and the Churches have strong channels of communication with policy makers and an important voice in consultations on policies that would affect them.

For more than half a century following the 1944 Act, state-funding of religious schools was restricted to the Christian and Jewish faiths. As new immigration led to a greater diversity of faith groups, the logic that these too should be part of the 1944 arrangements did not find favour with governments. Although newly arrived minority faith groups did open schools in the private sector, it was not until 1998 that the first state-funded Muslim school was approved.

Since then, the range of faiths represented in the state-funded sector has increased, with many independent faith schools transferring to the state sector as part of the academy programme. The framework that came into law in the 1944 Act to protect church schools now provides the legal framework for academies and Free Schools. It has given the present and the last Government the flexibility it needed to introduce a diversity of providers into the state-school system. The result has been not only an increase in the number of state-funded faith schools, but an increase in the number of faiths that are now providers of schools. In 2012, there were:

4598 Church of England Schools
1985 Roman Catholic Schools
  26 Methodist Schools
 142 Other Christian Schools
  41 Jewish Schools
  12 Muslim Schools
   9 Sikh Schools, and
   9 others including – Seventh Day Adventist, Quaker, United Reform and Greek Orthodox Schools (DfE).

The Arguments For and Against Faith Schools

Despite the long history of faith-based education in this country, it has never been without its critics. Yet, for decades, the different views rarely occupied centre stage. The past few years have seen that change. The present political and social context has led to challenging questions about some of the assumptions that underpin the role of faith groups, and voices for a secular school system have grown in strength.

The arguments for faith schools essentially remain the same. We are a society that claims to value religious freedom. A state-school system built on parental choice should not exclude the right of a parent to educate their child in the faith of their choice. The evidence shows that parents are attracted to faith schools, not just because of the tenets of the religion they preach but also because of the values that underpin them. Many parents who practise a faith would sooner send their child to a school of a different faith than to a non-faith school. If these arguments are not persuasive, faith schools can claim a role in historically educating the poor and protecting minorities. Some families from ethnic minorities argue that their children underperform in non-faith schools and that their needs can be better met by people who understand their cultural and religious background.

The arguments against faith schools also remain unchanged. Educating children of different religious beliefs separately leads to segregated communities and fosters a lack of religious understanding and tolerance. Faith groups should have the freedom to practise and promote their beliefs, but that should be done outside the structures of the formal education system. An absence of faith schools would not remove the freedom of parents to educate their children in a particular faith.

Both sides of the argument make a defensible case. Yet, the current debate about faith schools has gone beyond these boundaries. In particular, two new arguments have emerged. First, the claim that faith schools achieve higher standards of education, and second, that whatever the original purpose of faith schools, they are now socially selective and lead to greater segregation.

A debate around these two concerns is very much a debate of our times. Society has never needed or expected such high standards of education as it does from the present generation of young people. At a time when there is huge pressure on the school system to raise standards for all children, any group of schools that can claim to be doing better than others will be the focus of interest. Indeed, the belief that church schools outperform other schools was one of the reasons given by Tony Blair for the expansion of the Voluntary Aided model.

What does the evidence tell us about this? It is the case that overall, children in faith schools perform better at GCSE. However, this difference can be mainly accounted for by the background of the pupils who attend those schools. The evidence shows that faith schools, on average, recruit children from less socially disadvantaged backgrounds. This differs between the different faith groups (Rogers, 2012). Yet, success breeds success and the growing reputation of church schools has led to an increase in the number of applications and greater competition to secure a place. The overlap between selection by faith and selection by social class has been, in some cases, too close for comfort, and the tightening of the admissions code of practice is essential to guard against this. It is hard therefore to make the case, from the available evidence, that there is anything inherent in faith schools that leads to higher standards. The characteristics of outstanding schools – strong leadership, excellent teachers and high ambitions – can be found in any category of school.

The Impact of Faith Schools Within Mixed Faith Communities

The more pressing question is the role of faith schools in already fragmented communities. The social, political and economic circumstances of our times define this debate. More parents want a faith-school education for their child; more faiths want schools. Whereas historically, even those people who would not choose a faith-based school have been tolerant of other people's right to do so, they find their tolerance stretched now that a wider range of faith groups can run schools. Whatever view you have on the way the country has responded to the post-war multi-cultural society, there is widespread concern that we have become more segregated by religion and culture. Many urban areas have pockets of mono-culturalism adjacent to a pocket of another mono-culture.

There is a real concern that faith schools will yet further divide communities at a time when we need to build bridges. There is a fear that rather than bringing children from different back-grounds together, schools are becoming places that keep them apart. Wouldn't it have been better, people wonder, if Protestant and Catholic children in Northern Ireland had gone to school together? Wouldn't our understanding of the different cultures that now make up the country be better if children were educated alongside each other?

It is an argument that deserves serious debate. As the number of faith schools has expanded, there has probably been more religious segregation in their admissions. There are a great many

Church of England schools, but they often admit people from a range of faiths. That is not as true for Roman Catholic, Muslim, Sikh or other faith schools. Should these changes affect the age-old partnership between Church and State in the running of our schools? Perhaps the issue needs to be put in the context of a wider debate about society.

It is not just segregated schools that should worry us. The Cantle report said that 'distinct ethnic or religious communities can live within metres of each other without developing cultural or social bonds' (ICOCO, 2001). There are factors beyond education that are responsible for segregated communities. Lord Herman Ouseley talked about 'virtual apartheid between schools' in his report following the riots in Bradford, and in this case he was referring to schools, the majority of which weren't faith schools (Ouseley and ICOCO, 2001).

It can certainly be argued that a socially segregated school system would exist even without faith schools. The English school system is segregated by social class, with an independent sector that is too expensive for most people to access and state schools that often reflect the wealth of their neighbourhood. In some inner-city non-faith schools, almost all the school population are from ethnic minority religions, reflecting the population of the area in which the school is situated rather than the designation of the school. It has not needed faith schools to create an education system separated by religion. Even if state funding of faith schools was abolished, there would still be a strong independent sector; the percentage of schools in this group which are faith based is over 40 per cent.

If faith schools are not the main cause of social segregation, however, it does not absolve the education system from examining the role it plays. We need our schools to be forces for understanding, for teaching tolerance, for broadening horizons and building bridges. If faith schools can contribute to this, then they become a force for a strong society and not a divided one.

Government has opened the debate about the role faith schools might play and there have been a number of policy initiatives from governments of all parties. The present government has introduced a limit of 50 per cent in terms of the percentage of pupils whom Free Schools are allowed to admit with reference to their faith but whether they are likely to make it a requirement of all faith-based schools remains to be seen. The last government introduced a requirement on schools to foster community cohesion, and they were inspected on their progress as part of the Ofsted framework. There has been a call for better quality religious education and a broader religious curriculum in faith schools, and there is an on-going debate about admissions to faith schools. It is open to question whether these sorts of initiatives can address the concerns that are expressed by critics of faith schools.

Conclusion

At the heart of this debate is a question that returns to the central purpose of a faith-based education. Is the aim to create a school based on a particular set of values or one based on a particular set of religious beliefs? Many people who support faith schools do so because they believe them to be places of strong values with a shared understanding about the sort of society we should be. The schools argue that their faith gives them the guidance and confidence to be sure of the values that underpin what they do. This is what many parents are choosing when they select a faith school.

This is rather different from offering an education, the main purpose of which is to promote a particular set of beliefs. How this aspect of the debate develops seems to me to be the next stage in the long history of the relationship between faith groups and the State. It is important to defend faith-based schools on the more straightforward grounds of freedom and tolerance. However, like all institutions, faith schools need to respond to legitimate concerns in a fast-changing world.

We ought to recognize the role faith groups make in the education system but we should also expect to know what contribution they will make to educating a generation of young people who will achieve greater cohesion, understanding and solidarity than the generation who have gone before them.

Bibliography

Department for Education (DfE), 2012, *Schools, Pupils and their Characteristics: January 2012*, Ref. SFR10/2012, released 21 June 2012, available at http://www.education.gov.uk/rsgateway/DB/SFR/s001071/index.shtml.

Gerald Grace, 2002, *Catholic Schools: Missions, Market and Morality*, Oxford: Routledge.

Institute of Community Cohesion (ICOCO), 2001, *The Cantle Report – Community Cohesion: a report of the Independent Review Team*, published January 2001, available at http://resources.cohesioninstitute. org.uk/Publications/Documents/Document/Default.aspx?recordId=96.

Herman Ouseley and ICOCO, 2001, *The Ouseley Report: Community pride not prejudice – making diversity work in Bradford*, published January 2001, available at http://resources.cohesioninstitute.org.uk/ Publications/Documents/Document/Default.aspx?recordId=98.

Simon Rogers, 2012, 'How many poor children go to faith schools?' in *The Guardian Datablog*, 5 March 2012, available at http://www.guardian. co.uk/news/datablog/2012/mar/05/faith-schools-admissions.

10

Religion, Secularism and the Public Square

TONY BAYFIELD

At Home Yet Not at Home

When I originally gave the lecture on which this chapter was based, I felt completely at home speaking in Ripon Cathedral. I found the place wonderful, not just historically and aesthetically but spiritually. I was moved, uplifted. I was at home there, yet not at home – a metaphor for Jews like me in Britain today. Comfortable, at home, yet not simply at home; integrated but not assimilated; fully part of, yet creatively maladjusted (a phrase borrowed from the American Reform Jewish theologian Eugene B. Borowitz). When people are being nice to me, accepting me for who I am, respecting my particularism as well as my universalism, valuing my distinctiveness as well as celebrating our profound commonality, I would not be in any other place in the world than Britain or have it any other way. What this being at-home-yet-not-at-home means is that I see Britain affirmatively but through eyes that are different from those of Christians. My lenses are neither better nor worse, just distinctive. I hope that this essay does not turn out to be gratuitously provocative, only helpful as a perspective.

Judaism, Religion and Politics

I came relatively late to the subject of religion and contemporary Western political philosophy, via John Rawls and his contemporaries. I was brought up on the prophetic tradition of the Hebrew Bible, in which social and political engagement are what religion is all about. That tradition finds the distinction between the public and the private incomprehensible. I am not ashamed to say, that, at Cambridge, I may have read Law but thought seriously of going into politics. In the end, I went to the Leo Baeck College in London to study to be a rabbi and undertook five years of rigorous, full-time learning. But consciously, because I saw politics as a system for putting values into social action, what I wanted to do was to grapple with the source of my values – Judaism – and contribute to society in that way.

My current preoccupation with religion and the State can be traced back to a book I have been working on, contributing to and co-editing over the past three years (Bayfield, Race and Siddiqui, eds, 2012). It is a book that has emerged from more than a decade of dialogue between a group of Jews, Christians and Muslims. The book is about how we need to change in order to resume our place within the public square, a place we have abdicated to the strident voices of fundamentalism, religious and secular. It is equally about how government and society need to change in order to make that resumption possible. Three years of working on the book have made me very aware of the phrase 'public square'. I have been looking for it ever since. My search is the tenuous thread that runs through this chapter.

I now realize that my interest in the relationship between religion and modern Western, liberal democracy goes back a lot further than my Jewish–Christian–Muslim book. It goes back to a revelation that stemmed from an earlier dialogue experience. It is fascinating how much of the thinking most precious to me arises out of inter-faith dialogue rather than internal Jewish debate. That earlier dialogue group was a Jewish–Christian one and its decade of work also ended with a book (Bayfield and Braybrooke, eds, 1992). The closing chapter, by the distinguished Orthodox rabbi Norman Solomon, was entitled 'The Third Presence: Reflections on the Dialogue'. The third presence, said Norman Solomon, was 'the civilization of modernity, or of enlightenment' (Solomon in Bayfield and Braybrooke, p. 148). Whenever, Solomon pointed

out in true Solomonic fashion, Christians and Jews talk together
in Britain today, a third partner is always present. That third
presence is the culture in which we are educated, live and breathe,
which he called modernity, enlightenment. The penny dropped.
For me, but of course not for Christians, the starting point was
neither the search for the public square, nor even the revelation
that the third dialogue partner, modernity, is always present in
our lives. My starting point as a Jew is the Enlightenment with a
capital 'E' – the emergence of the Jews of Western Europe from
the ghettos in which they had been confined until the beginning
of the nineteenth century: their confrontation with a new culture,
the world of the Enlightenment, Western civilization, modernity.
That is where my pre-occupation with religion and the State
actually starts.

Modern Western Culture

It is on this Western culture that I now focus. Jews began their
encounter with today's global mega-culture at the end of the
eighteenth and the beginning of the nineteenth centuries. But, of
course, the party was already in full swing when Moses Mendels-
sohn (1729–86) made his way to Berlin. As an aside and a gross
over-simplification – but then I have spent much of my career
giving sermons so I am totally committed to the use of gross over-
simplification – Judaism was largely undifferentiated until that
point. We had not then fully learned the art of doctrinal rivalry
and internecine warfare that characterized the Reformation. But
we soon caught up and have, sadly, not outgrown it today.

Jews reacted in all sorts of ways to the wonderlands of French,
German and Austro-Hungarian culture. Some threw off their
shabby Jewish gabardine and raced to embrace Christianity.
Others stood in shock and horror, before resolutely turning their
backs both spiritually and intellectually in order to preserve the
familiar, the life they thought they had always known. I come from
an intermediate stream which saw both dazzling opportunity and
terrifying challenge, wobbled, steadied itself and came very slowly

to realize that this was and is just the next stage on that remarkable journey which goes back to Sinai. I write, of course, with the benefit of two hundred years of hindsight, selecting what I want to acknowledge from what I would prefer to forget. But for me – in retrospect, in the here and now and in prospect – my Judaism is about accepting the terrain – *ich kann nicht anders*, to quote the eminent anti-Semite Martin Luther – both for its benefits and for its challenges, recognizing that while there are many seductive, destructive voices there is also revelation in modernity.

Revelation in Modernity

What am I talking about when I say revelation in modernity? I return to my at-home-yet-not-at-homeness, my creative maladjustment, my different, or better, distinctive perspective. Personally, I feel immensely liberated by having learned that what I call Torah, and others call the Five Books of Moses, is not extra-historical, is not God's literal word sent whizzing through outer space to be transcribed verbatim at Sinai. Torah is our ancestors' perception of God and a record of revelation as they grasped it, with all their human genius and human limitations. I am immensely relieved that I do not have to believe in what is utterly contrary to both historical and personal experience – in a God who zaps the wicked and rescues the good. I welcome enthusiastically the spiritual, theological and intellectual insights and challenges that are explicit in modernity. Of course I am also deeply fearful. You have no idea what it is like to be part of a people of whom there are only 14 million in the world and 267,000 in Britain. It is not funny being a member of an endangered species and it could well be that this modernity which I embrace will, in fact, wipe out the Jewish people. But we progressive Jews journey on and try not to make the same mistake as Lot's wife of looking back.

Modernity and Secularity

Which leads me to the first major point I have been reaching for – the authorship and ownership of this culture within which all of us live and breathe – and feel both at home in and not at home in. Norman Solomon called it modernity. But in so much of the reading that I have done over the past couple of years – looking at how others regard the terrain through which we people of faith find ourselves journeying – it seems most frequently to be called secular; modern secular culture.

One of the teachers to whom I owe most is the Anglican theologian and publisher, John Bowden, who died in 2010. Using the university as his yardstick, Bowden traced the rise of secularism and saw the tipping point in European history as the Peace of Westphalia in 1648. The Peace of Westphalia can be seen as the point at which political power moved from the Church to 'the Princes'. That is a very significant shift – from the Lords Spiritual to the Lords Temporal – but it is not the same as a complete cultural shift from a holy religious world view to a wholly secular world view. It is part of a much more complex cultural development. By secularism, however, Bowden does not mean implacable opposition to a religious world view. He means this complex culture which first dazzled Jews 200 years ago, this dominant mega-culture which has now gone global.

That culture, our culture, the third dialogue partner, owes a lot to a lot of people. It owes much to Greece and Rome. It owes much to the emergence of modern science. It owes much to the theorists of the French and American Revolutions. But it also owes a huge amount to the Judaeo-Christian tradition or traditions, depending upon whether you see that tradition as homogenous or bifurcating eighteen centuries ago. Of course, it includes a profound critique of religion, particularly as religion once was (and of which religious fundamentalists provide a cruel pastiche). Of course, it contains bleak, nihilistic, super-rationalist dimensions that are non-comprehending of religion and offer it no place. Finally, of course, secularism, defined as having no religious world view, is a part of modernity. But, from my Jewish perspective, modernity is much, much richer and more interesting than that. The elision of modern, Western culture and secularism is false. They are not the same. Having come to that conclusion, I now realize I cannot see the public square because what others have defined as the public square is now under occupation. I will return later to who is occupying this public square.

Secularism in Two Guises

Before returning to the public square, there are two trends, clearly connected, which I want, nevertheless, to separate out. The world has witnessed the rise and rise of fundamentalism since the 1960s. Whenever I use the term fundamentalist, hackles rise; first because the term originated in America to describe a Christian phenomenon which, back in the first decade of the twentieth century, had no obvious parallel in Judaism. Secondly, and much more importantly, because people think that I am attacking lovely, cuddly people, steeped in wisdom and integrity, who have withdrawn from these difficult times in order to go back to past authenticity and simplicity.

I am not quite sure what that evasion is about. However, drawing on the work of the American scholar Martin Marty and his studies on fundamentalism, I am referring solely and exclusively to those whose fundamental beliefs have been shaken by the challenges of modern thought, who have responded by turning their back on the challenge, attempted to recreate a past world that never actually existed, who re-assert the old and shaken truths in a simplistic and banal way, believe themselves to be the sole possessors of Truth and seek to impose that Truth on others, by force if necessary. It is what the British Catholic scholar Peter Vardy has termed 'bad religion' (Vardy, 2010). It rears its ugly head in many of the world's most tragic and violent situations. It discredits good religion, causes untold misery to humanity and disfigures the globe. The phenomenon is to be found particularly – not exclusively, but shamefully – in Judaism, Christianity and Islam, the three Abrahamic faiths. What many of us are guilty of

is not having done enough to oppose and condemn fundamentalist manifestations within our own faiths. We therefore have to
accept a considerable responsibility for the rise and rise of secular
fundamentalism, which seeks to present religion as a wholly – or
rather unholy – malign influence, and which is hysterically and
neurotically dismissive of all religion.

But there is something else going on, something other than the
rise of hubristic religious fundamentalism and strident secular
fundamentalism. That is why I was so struck by Michael Sandel's
2009 Reith Lectures and his book *Justice* (Sandel, 2009). Sandel,
who is Professor of Government at Harvard, demonstrates the
extent to which American public life is under the continuing
domination of Jeremy Bentham, utilitarianism and the principle
of the greatest happiness of the greatest number. According to the
neo-Benthamites, the task of government and public institutions
– including the law – is not to get side-tracked into irrational,
subjective discussions about values but simply to work for the
greatest happiness of the greatest number. Sandel goes on to
describe the major, competing view of the last half of the twentieth
century – that the aim of government, public institutions, the law,
is to maximize not happiness but individual freedom. By which
is meant, at bottom, economic freedom. For many decades, the
guru of this view was the aforementioned John Rawls, Professor
of Moral and Political Philosophy, once again at Harvard. Rawls
tempered the absolute of maximizing freedom with the need to
ameliorate the situation of the economically underprivileged. So
he coupled liberty with economic justice.

Sandel is critical of both Bentham and Rawls. He invokes
Aristotle and the view that in the good society, a range of ethical
values is essential. He writes: 'Debates about justice and rights are
often, unavoidably, debates about the purpose of social institutions, the goods they allocate, and the virtues they honour and
reward. Despite our best attempts to make law neutral on such
questions, it may not be possible to say what's just without arguing about the nature of the good life' (Sandel, p. 207). Too right
it is not possible! As key elements of public policy, justice and
law are central and integral to the creation of the good life for the

individual and the society we strive to create. But let us be clear. 'The good life' is not a reference to a 1970s sit-com about returning to the soil in rural South West London. It is Aristotle's vision for society. Sixteenth- and seventeenth-century Jewish mystics, among whom the key figure for me is Isaac Luria, who was born in 1534 in Jerusalem, understood that in every situation and relationship there are sparks of goodness waiting to be released. Our task in life, they urged, is to release those sparks, to increase the fund of good in the world. Life is not just about the maximization of individual liberty and the pursuit of happiness for the majority. The mainstream Jewish view is that we live in order to realize the good for God's sake and for everyone else's as well. One of the things that I find interesting about Sandel is that, although he is Jewish, I do not think that the word religion, let alone Judaism, appears in his book at all. The nature of justice and its contribution to society is solely a secular, philosophical matter to which Judaism and Christianity appear to have nothing to contribute.

Offering a different approach is a lengthy study *The Idea of Justice* by Amartya Sen. Sen is one of the great polymaths of our times, Indian by cultural inheritance, Oxbridge by employment. Sen, who won the Nobel Prize for Economics in 1998, is a distinguished philosopher and, in 2009, published a *magnum opus* on justice and the principles by which public life and public institutions should be governed. He is more forthright even than Sandel in dismissing the greatest happiness of the greatest number as the governing principle. At first, he is extremely complimentary about his deceased friend John Rawls, and then demolishes the man's life's work with unfailingly polite but ruthless forensic skill.

Sen makes the attention-grabbing point, which shook me at first, of condemning Bentham and Rawls and their followers for 'looking for a metaphysic'. Sen looks again and again for ways in which values and external perspectives can be injected into a pragmatic and down-to-earth enterprise, making an unjust society that little bit more just. I slowly realized that what Sen was dismissing as a metaphysic was the pursuit of a Platonic ideal, an overarching principle from which everything else logically descends – such as the greatest happiness or individual liberty.

Sen urges us to get on with the daily work in a way which Judaism calls *tikkun olam*, the repair of the world, 'patching up the world and making it work' a little better, to quote Rabbi Lionel Blue (Blue, 1975, p. 102).

Secularism in the Mainstream and the Christian Response

Without doubt 'something else is going on' beside the shouting match between those with their ears shut tight, the religious and secular fundamentalists. There is a process in hand that is far more challenging to religion and far more subversive of our role in society than the secular fundamentalism of which the flag bearers have been Richard Dawkins and the late Christopher Hitchens.

I recently came across a very long essay – if it had been fiction I would have called it a novella – by Jonathan Chaplin (2008). Chaplin is Director of the Kirby Laing Institute for Christian Ethics at Cambridge. The essay is a defence of bringing religion and God into public debate. It is very well argued and deals with a range of issues relating to public reasoning, which was a term I was scarcely aware of. Public reasoning is what goes on in that public square which I have still not found! What became apparent to me, reading Chaplin, was that Christianity in Britain is very much on the defensive when it comes to Christian reasoning and Christian justification of views and opinions advanced in public institutions and public life. The defensiveness, it seems to me as a maladjusted Jew, has its roots in the distinctively Christian notion of doctrine and the way doctrine has been (mis)used in public debate. So, quoting Janet Daley writing in *The Daily Telegraph* in 2008: 'In the contest between the principles of modern democracy and doctrines of faith, democracy and the rule of secular law must always win' (Chaplin p. 13).

Chaplin, thankfully, argues that people of faith can legitimately invoke their faith in public debate. He draws on a distinction made by the former Archbishop of Canterbury Rowan Williams between 'programmatic secularism' and 'procedural secularism'. Programmatic secularism intentionally imposes a secularist faith on the public realm and works to privatize religious faith as much as possible. Procedural secularism seeks to allow all faith perspectives equal access to the public realm but claims to confer no political privilege on any. So programmatic secularism – 'We secularists have the only legitimate voice in public debate; you Christians should shut up. Go and talk to yourselves in your churches, behind closed doors' – is to be resisted and opposed. But procedural secularism is legitimate. All faiths having equal access to the public square but not seeking a special political privilege over secular voices is music to my ears. But why is it called procedural secularism? Why is reasoned debate in the public square procedural *secularism*? There are echoes here of a helpful debate initiated by the German philosopher Jürgen Habermas. Nevertheless both Christianity and Judaism are heavily invested in the Western philosophical tradition of reason and logic.

Chaplin worries about how Christians set about justifying their views. He focuses on what he regards as the ultimate justification, 'Because Jesus is Lord', and agonizes about whether not using that formulation – which is heard by others as playing a trump card, vetoing further discussion – calls into question the integrity of the Christian argument. To my relief, he comes to the conclusion that secularists are not only wrong in trying to exclude Christians from the public debate, but that it is fine for Christians to use 'secular reasoning' and not explicitly play the 'Because Jesus is Lord' card.

What strikes me, as the Jew new to all this and looking through my at-home-but-not-at-home lens, is the following: first, we do not live in a secular society. We live in a society the culture of which is rich, diverse, and pluralistic. Secularism, defined as rejecting a religious view of the world, is only a part of it. It is a vociferous part but manifestly, unarguably only a part. So why be so apologetic and defensive? Second, secularists – in advancing principles such as 'the task of government is to achieve the greatest happiness of the greatest number' or 'public institutions should be neutral, framed only by the principle of maximizing individual liberty insofar as it is consonant with economic justice' – are actually in much the same territory as religions. Those are very important and interesting principles, hypotheses. But that is all they are; they ultimately rest on belief.

Third, as a Jew, I am part of a very small minority. It is therefore axiomatic for me to use language that people will understand if, as I do, I want to contribute to the public debate. It is no betrayal of the God of Abraham and Sarah that I do not pepper public debate with Hebrew. Even though God speaks *lashon ha'kodesh*, the holy tongue, not using Hebrew does not tarnish my integrity. I need to speak in the 'language of human beings' as early rabbinic teaching emphasized the Torah was written in, the lingua franca of society. Furthermore, if the lingua franca of society, particularly public debate, calls for reason, then reason I will use. Louis Jacobs called his best known and most influential book *We Have Reason to Believe*. Rabbi Dr Jacobs, perhaps British Jewry's finest scholar of the twentieth century, used reason without ever believing that it was secular. The Christian philosopher Aquinas used reason. The Jewish philosopher Maimonides used reason. Why are we surrendering reason to the secularists?

Fourth, the emphasis on doctrine is actually a feature of Christianity and, in particular, of post-Reformation Christianity. To which Christianity is perfectly entitled, but which gets up the noses of secularists in a way that, dare I say it, may not be strategically sensible. Chaplin sympathizes with 'those who insist on always making the evangelical content of the doctrine clear, not veiling it in embarrassment' (Chaplin, p. 34). But it seems to me – as an impertinent Jewish outsider – that as the largest and most important faith voice in Britain, Christianity in the market place may need to speak the language of the market place and rely on the undoubted quality of the spiritual, intellectual and ethical fruits on offer to sell itself. Finally, in my humble opinion, the besetting sin of all religions is a lack of humility. The truth claims that we make manage to combine both hubris and absurdity. That is something I have often said. But only at this point did I realize that secularists – whether they be secular fundamentalists or, to use Chaplin's term, liberal-secularists – share that same besetting sin. This is not a call for philosophical or moral relativism, but simply a plea for humility, for listening to each other and being prepared to learn from each other. Dismissing religion as having nothing to say that ordinary mortals can understand and as pre-empting rational debate by always using a metaphysical veto are both inexcusably arrogant non-arguments.

Where is the Public Square?

At this point, it would be useful to summarize. I have argued that we live within a rich, diverse and pluralistic culture to which Jews and Christians have made an enormous contribution. It is not a secular society. Not so long ago we, the Abrahamic faiths, sought to dominate and control society. Proponents of secularism, not the wild men but sober political philosophers and thinkers, for admittedly understandable reasons, have gone a long way in putting us on the defensive and supplanting us. But why should we be supplanted? We have just as much right and just as great a duty to play a part in the public square as they have. Which leads me to the final part of my argument, which is: 'where *is* that damned public square that everyone, including me, talks about but I cannot find?'

At long last, the penny has finally dropped and I realize that it is presently located in Westminster and what used to be called Fleet Street. Chaplin identifies Parliament and the press as the two most important locations and the only ones he names. They are the places currently under secularist occupation; where programmatic secularism has really put us on the defensive if not to flight. At this point I become conscious that I am about to utter an outrageous piece of *chutzpah*. But I have to say it. There lies our mistake. Walter Bagehot is not my favourite constitutionalist. But Bagehot is the source of one of the most brilliant insights into the nature of democracy. Democracy, says Bagehot, is not the tyranny of majoritarianism. Democracy is discussion, and debate (Bagehot cited in Sen, p. 3).

Although Parliament thrives on debate and is one of the places where debate takes place, government and Parliament have an overriding function, which is to take forward, advance and build the kind of society that society in the public square has broadly agreed on. Parliament is the place where the vision is implemented not where it is thrashed out in all its essential detail. This presents us with an apparent problem because it would seem that the vision for British society is not shared today. Sandel questions the Benthamite vision of a society in which the greatest number experience the greatest happiness. Sen challenges the Rawlians vision of individual freedom coupled with economic justice. Peter Vardy puts his faith in Aristotle because, he says, Aristotle appeals to theists and atheists alike. Vardy envisages a society in which each individual can flourish. I, for myself, would talk about the good life, meaning life in which goodness is maximized. I would equate that with a society in which justice and compassion are supreme.

In present reality rather than in abstract philosophical theory, these ideals do not sit so badly together. More importantly, let us just go back to my initial shock at Amartya Sen's rejection of what he called metaphysics and which turned out to mean a Platonic ideal, a governing philosophical principle like the four I have just spelled out. I was shocked at first but I now think that Sen is absolutely right. Sen argues for a much more pragmatic approach, trying to make our society and the world a little bit more just. That resonates strongly with me as a Jew, wedded to the concept of repair, of patching and mending and improving little by little. What is just, what is fair, what is good in any given situation cannot be decided by putting the case through a computer programmed to apply the greatest happiness of the greatest number, or individual freedom, to any given situation under examination. It demands debate and discussion which embrace a range of ethical perspectives. I believe, *pace* Alasdair MacIntyre (2007), it can be done at the national level, even in a diverse and pluralistic society like ours. But it can only be done through detailed discussion and debate on a case-by-case, instance-by-instance basis – in the public square. Parliament is not that public square because it does not have the time, because it is not broad enough but most of all because that is not its function. Its function is to input and consult, to listen and implement, to increase happiness, advance freedom, enable the individual to flourish, build the good society founded on justice and compassion.

The debate cannot take place exclusively in the press either – because the task of the press is to provide us with news, to inform and, inevitably, to simplify and even to sensationalize in order to capture our attention. The task of the press is not to supply acres of print devoted to detailed discussion of the values which should regulate free markets or constrain unbridled scientific research. Nor is it even to report, Hansard-like, the debate, the discussion which is, back to Bagehot, the real meaning of democracy – a debate, a discussion in which I as a Jew and many Christians want to take part or at least be adequately represented. We need to further develop the public square in this country. We need to institutionalize it so that the religious and the secular can share insights and reasoned argument about those many, many subjects which are relevant to the flourishing of individuals and the society in which the individual can flourish. Britain needs a public square where, as Rowan Williams argues, the faiths have equal access to the public realm but claim no particular, special privileges (Williams cited in Chaplin, p. 21).

The Public Square as a Challenge to the Faiths

I want to end by posing three questions. They are largely rhetorical questions to which I think I already know the answers. But what else would you expect from a member of the clergy who preaches humility!

First, can we, members of the Abrahamic faiths, recognize that being on occasions in the minority is inevitable if the plurality of voices in our culture are to be given genuine respect? Can we teach one thing to members of our own faith community and allow the rest of society – after due discussion in the public square – to take a different path, for instance, over assisted suicide? Second, do we need our own space in which we are permitted to depart from the democratically established cultural consensus? A Jewish example might be over infant circumcision. But should there also be limits to our space? For instance, over issues such as the full equality of women or the rights of gays and lesbians?

Third, and slightly differently, religions today, in some sense at least, are all minorities in Britain. But what follows has particular implications for minority faiths and newer immigrant groups. We aspire to be multi-identity citizens, participating fully in the modern, Western, liberal democracy that is Britain. Would it be helpful for there to be *res publica* contracts in which society covenants to respect and protect our rights to be who we are and to practise our faiths according to their unique configuration and rhythm? And should we covenant to respect the government of our society – and its modern, liberal, democratic character – as it pursues the just and compassionate society in which each equal individual can flourish?

Being heard, having access to the public square and making good use of that access, contributing with reason, sensitivity and humility to the public debate – that is the very essence of democracy. We people of faith can be faithful democrats just as much as the divines of secularity. It is true that – given the vast Christian contribution to Britain – that may feel slightly strange to many Christians. But at-home-yet-not-quite-at-home, creatively maladjusted – perhaps that is how it should feel for all the children of Abraham and Sarah?

Bibliography

Tony Bayfield and Marcus Braybrooke (eds), 1992, *Dialogue with a Difference*, London: SCM Press.

Tony Bayfield, Alan Race and Ataullah Siddiqui (eds), 2012, *Beyond the Dysfunctional Family*, London: Manor House Dialogue Group.

Lionel Blue, 1975, *To Heaven with Scribes and Pharisees: The Jewish Path to God*, London: Darton, Longman & Todd.

Jonathan Chaplin, 2008, *Talking God: The Legitimacy of Religious Public Reasoning*, London: Theos.

Janet Daley, 2008, 'Removing the state from Dr Rowan Williams', *The Daily Telegraph*, 11 February.

Louis Jacobs, 1957, 1995, *We Have Reason to Believe*, 4th revised edition, London: Vallentine Mitchell.

Alasdair MacIntyre, 2007, *After Virtue*, 3rd edition, London: Duckworth.
Michael J. Sandel, 2009, *Justice: What's the Right Thing to Do*, London: Allen Lane.
Amartya Sen, 2009, *The Idea of Justice*, London: Allen Lane.
Peter Vardy, 2010, *Good and Bad Religion*, London: SCM Press.

Conclusion

Why *Should* People Go to Church?

NICHOLAS BUXTON

The essays in this volume clearly show not only that the 'question of God' remains pertinent, if contested, but also that faith continues to play a significant role in many aspects of public life in Britain today, even if its influence is not always favourably regarded. Indeed, public expressions of religious identity and the role of religious institutions are coming under increasing – and sometimes critical – scrutiny, whether that be in relation to the wearing of religious insignia at work, the status of 'faith schools', or the place of Anglican bishops in the House of Lords. As Roger Trigg points out, recent legal cases seem to suggest that the right to freedom of religion may be compromised or overruled by other rights, especially those guaranteed by equality legislation, on the debatable assumption that religion is a choice, whereas gender or sexuality are not.

There appears to be a strongly secularist bias evident in much public discourse, and widely propagated by the media, which implicitly – and sometimes explicitly – regards religion as an irrational superstition that incites conflict and division. Thus it should be denied any part in determining public policy or shaping social norms, and can only be tolerated so long as it is confined to the private sphere. However, these attitudes ignore certain important facts about religion. To begin with, there is no such thing as private religion, just as there is no such thing as a truly neutral secular space. Religious convictions, privately held, require from the believer public expression, or as Mona Siddiqui puts it, 'Belief in God demands an obligation to talk of God' (pages 35–6).

Moreover, the repression of religious perspectives in the public domain implicitly rejects the possibility that religion may actually have something positive to contribute to the common good. Yet, as Catherine Pepinster argues, Christian teaching 'makes the case for policies and practices that above all respect the dignity and worth of each person' (page 107).

Whatever one's views on the place of religion in public life, it would certainly seem to be the case that, in this part of the world at least, many institutional forms of religion – particularly the mainstream Christian Churches – are in decline. Even nominal Christian identification has fallen sharply, as the 2011 census results show, against a corresponding rise in the number of people declaring themselves as having 'no religion'. Having said that, however, the waning social significance of religious institutions does not appear to have resulted in the disappearance of what one might describe as humanity's innate religious instincts. Far from it. Religion, or at least the purpose it serves, remains a human and social constant. The urges that people have sought to fulfil by recourse to religious faith and practice remain undiminished, even if the numbers involved in formal expressions of religious affiliation are much reduced. Just as people have physical needs, so they have needs that may be described as 'spiritual'. Moreover, in the absence of a common religious narrative, there are many diverse ways in which people seek to fulfil them. The only difference is that the Church, and the Christian world view it represents, is no longer considered normative with respect either to defining those needs or servicing them. This is why it is common to hear people talk about a widespread 'hunger for spirituality' – which is usually configured in opposition to so-called 'organized religion' – or to describe themselves as 'spiritual but not religious'.

The fact is we no longer live in a society in which the basic assumptions of the Christian world view, or that of any other religion, can be taken for granted. Furthermore, challenges to faith come not only from outside but also from within religious traditions. To give two very different examples, Dan Cohn-Sherbok and Daphne Hampson both grapple with the need to find justifiable ways to speak meaningfully of God in a post-Holocaust and post-feminist context respectively. Our changing socio-cultural landscape compels churches and other faith groups to navigate carefully between responding to culture and reacting against it, or between adapting to society and assimilating to it. This raises difficult questions for faith leaders to which there are seldom easy answers. Social change cannot be ignored, but at the same time it would be naïve to suppose that as long as the essence of the tradition is maintained, there can be a degree of flexibility about the cultural forms in which it is expressed. What is the essence? And when is it ever independent of its manifestation in a particular context? In such circumstances, it is hardly surprising that missionary discourses should feature so prominently in church life. In many Church of England dioceses, for example, parishes are encouraged to draw up a 'Mission Action Plan', an enterprise that is often driven by an explicit 'growth agenda'. Therefore, in concluding this volume of essays on religion, society and God, I will offer some thoughts on Christian mission in a culture in which the basic suppositions of a Christian – or even simply religious – world view can no longer be taken for granted.

Christians believe that God is love, and that he calls us to participate in his divine mission by making that love manifest among us. This is the 'new commandment' instituted by Jesus: 'Just as I have loved you, you also should love one another' (John 13.34 NRSV). Mission is no more – nor less – than our duty to make God's love known in the world. In spite of this unequivocal mandate, however, it is not always clear what people really mean when they talk about mission, which often tends to get confused with evangelism or apologetics. Strictly speaking, 'mission' refers to God's mission of love, in which we are all called to participate by loving our neighbour. Evangelism, on the other hand, which could be seen as a particular expression of mission, is essentially the work of nurturing disciples, whilst apologetics is concerned with articulating rational justifications for religious faith and doctrine. Mission is thus about the service of the Church to the world. Yet there appears – perhaps inevitably – to be a strongly evangelistic, and at times apologetic, emphasis in much of what is called mission, which nowadays seems primarily to focus on efforts to get more people to come to church, rather than on making God known in the world by realizing his Kingdom. Of course, these objectives may be connected, but it does nevertheless sometimes seem that filling the building is considered more important than building community.

It is often, and rightly, argued that whatever else may be involved, mission can only begin by meeting people where they are – as Paul did in Athens – and engaging with them in terms they can relate to (Acts 17.17, 22–8). But beyond this simple analysis, things start to get more complicated. How are religious institutions to engage with people in a society that lacks a common religious vocabulary, and in which the validity and value of religion itself is called into question? The Pauline approach is often taken to mean we need to find new ways of telling the old story, and indeed at their ordination, priests are exhorted to 'proclaim the gospel afresh in every generation'. But it no longer seems sufficient – or even possible – to re-tell the story in more appealing or 'relevant' ways when that story is no longer part of everyday life. Many would concede that the moral truths contained in religious narratives have a perennial vitality, yet the overarching meta-narrative seems to be losing its purchase on the collective imagination. The Christian story is no longer deemed relevant or meaningful, it is no longer culturally normative, and so people increasingly tend not to comprehend their lives in relation to it. And the reason for this is presumably because they have lost any sense that these stories and the truths they contain are necessary, or even conducive, to human flourishing.

Generally speaking, the Church seems to understand mission in terms of making known the 'good news' of Jesus Christ. But herein lies a fundamental problem. In the world in which we live, good news just isn't *news*. This simple point highlights the enormous gap that exists between the Church and the world, and how each understands its relationship to the other. And because the Church seems unable to grasp the nature and extent of this disconnection, it is repeatedly accused of being out of touch. But instead of asking people what their actual spiritual needs are, the Church presumes that it already has the answer. Aware of the 'great spiritual hunger' in society, the Church assumes both that alternative forms of spirituality are bogus or defective and that it has a monopoly on the 'correct' form of spiritual nourishment. As a result, missionary discourse tends to begin from the unexamined assumption that people *should* go to church, the only question being how to get them through the doors. But *why* should they? It is taken for granted that they should, but it is never explained why this is the case. Note this is not the same as the more pragmatic question that asks, 'Why *do* people go to church?' The answers to that will be many and varied, and include aesthetic, social and habitual reasons among others. The question, rather, is why the existing churchgoer assumes that people who currently do not go to church *should* go to church.

In order to answer this, it may help to consider the purpose of religious adherence. After all, conscious identification with a religion presumably entails a compelling reason to think that such faith is worthwhile or necessary. One might, for example, argue that the fundamental motive underlying faith derives – whether consciously or not – from the realization that there is something profoundly unsatisfactory about the human condition, which in Christian terms would be described as the state of fallenness or 'original sin'. Thus the recognition that things are not as they should be leads to the awareness that we are in need of redemption, and therefore that we need to do something about it: we need to make the world a better place, and we need to start by making ourselves better people. In other words, a solution needs a problem. But instead of promoting clear reasons why people *should* go to church – instead of articulating the problem to which religion might be the solution – many churches seem to obsess about how to make their services more relevant and appealing, in the hope that a change of format will somehow make a difference.

And so, inevitably, the nagging question persists. Why do we assume that people should go to church in the first place? And then it suddenly clicked. Religion is really no different to any other business. Churches are simply trying to sell their wares. Moreover, they are all chasing after the same dwindling pool of 'customers' in an industry that, in this part of the world at least, is currently in severe, if not terminal, recession. Seen in terms of a market paradigm, churches behave just like any other organization, desperately trying to increase their customer base and market share.

At this juncture I should perhaps say a word about my deliberate use of market language. It is not that I have a background in commerce, nor that I am trying to be trendy or provocative. I am using the language of the market because that is – and probably always has been – the universal language of everyday life in the world in which we live. The point is simply that, as Tony Bayfield puts it, 'Christianity in the marketplace may need to speak the language of the marketplace' (page 147) After all, what is 'the market' other than the public domain, the place of exchange and interaction, not only of goods and services but also of ideas and culture, gossip and relationships? Commerce and communication are fundamentally similar activities. Of course, there are occasions when the Church must take a prophetic stand, and is surely right at times to challenge government policies or contradict societal norms. But in order to do this the Church must be in the market square in the first place, as Paul was in Athens, because that is the locus of society, and therefore the arena within which the Church needs to be active and engaged.

This is neither to suggest that churches should be run as businesses, nor that clergy should adopt managerial techniques and attitudes. The Church is not a business in all sorts of important ways, and it should go without saying that there are many business methods that would be inappropriate to a church context. In spite of that, however, there nevertheless appears to be a tendency for church leaders to 'buy into' market discourses, whether deliberately or not, presumably because such language permeates all aspects of everyday life. Evidence for this can be seen in the Church's obsession with growth – specifically numerical growth – whereby the 'success' of a church is measured in terms of quantitative rather than qualitative data. By internalizing the capitalist assumptions of the prevailing culture, however, the Church implicitly colludes with the marketization of human existence, and its Darwinian model of the survival of the fittest.

Indeed, the narrative of the market is now so all-pervasive that it is becoming almost impossible for us to think in any other terms. Therefore, if churches want to engage with the world, they would appear to have little choice but to accept its language. If they want to be more appealing to potential 'customers' then they need to understand the nature of the business they are in, and they need to understand their 'product'. What, to put it bluntly, are religious organizations 'selling'?

There could be a number of answers to this question, but for the sake of simplicity, let us say that the 'product' churches are 'selling' is salvation. Having identified the product, we then need to consider the 'market'. Even the briefest of surveys will no doubt indicate that salvation is likely to be a hard sell in a society that does not appear to consider the benefits and consolations of faith to be of any great value. The task for those in the religion business, then, is to persuade people that just as they need food and shelter, so they also need spiritual nourishment and sanctuary; and, moreover, that the Church has this to offer.

This should not be as difficult as it sometimes seems. In spite of all the evidence for declining church attendance, and widespread indifference to religion in general, there is also evidence that residual belief in God, or at least a spiritual dimension, remains the default position for the majority. Convinced atheists remain a small, if vocal, minority. Yet relatively few of the people who claim to believe in God seem willing to express this by being part of a worshipping community. In short, they do not see why they should go to church. Church represents something that is widely perceived to be boring, irrelevant and untrue. It does not appeal to them, it does not engage them, it does not meet their needs. In these circumstances, if the churches cannot provide an answer to the question of why people *should* go to church, they have little chance of changing the statistics.

Part of the problem may be that church actually *is* boring and irrelevant, compared with the standards and expectations people now have. Gone are the days when church was the best show in town, or the only thing to do on a Sunday. Much of what the Church used to provide, such as education and healthcare, has been professionalized. Its main rival, the entertainment industry, has grown exponentially, both in volume as well as sophistication. There are so many competing demands on our attention that churchgoing is just not a priority: there are simply better ways to spend one's time. This is why some people think that the Church needs to find new ways of telling the old stories, by adopting the motifs and technologies of contemporary culture. Yet, merely re-telling the story in a more contemporary idiom will not by itself make the story more relevant. To be more relevant, it has to relate to the actual needs and experiences of people's lives, not try to dictate them. It has to 'speak to their condition', not just appeal to their taste in music. Changing the means of communication, such as by singing songs by U2 instead of Victorian hymns, still fails to address the more fundamental question: why *should* people go to church in the first place? The glib – as well as true – answer might be because we are in need of salvation, but this only pushes the question one stage further back. Why are we in need of salvation? Without a clear account of what salvation means, and why we are in need of it, there is no apparent point to religion. If churches wish to increase their market share, then they need to be able to articulate good reasons for why people should 'invest' in them. If people 'need' to go to church because they are in need of salvation, then this is what needs to be explained. It requires not just a change of vocabulary, but a completely different language.

The St Wilfrid lectures at Ripon Cathedral, out of which this book has grown, began in 2009 with a series entitled, 'Rethinking Mission: the Role of the Church in Contemporary Society'. When churches ask themselves about mission, and how to be more relevant to people's lives, they should not be thinking about how to attract more people to services – such as by translating ancient liturgy into the vernacular of popular culture – but about how they can be of service to their community, be that the parish, civic society, or the workplace. The task facing ministers in the 'religion business' is to find ways of forging meaningful relationships with those whom they are called to serve. If mission is about making known the love of God in the world, then it consists not so much in winning arguments but making friends. It really is as simple as that. More often, however, it seems – to put it a little crudely – that mission is understood as having something to do with the question of how to get more people to come to church services. Both notions use the same word, 'service', but with very different connotations. Mission is not primarily about the 'growth agenda' – though few would deny that increased attendance would be a welcome by-product – but building community. Rather than asking, 'Why don't people come to our services?', churches should be asking, 'What service are we providing for the people among whom we find ourselves?'

Lightning Source UK Ltd.
Milton Keynes UK
UKOW03f1452030114

223924UK00005B/53/P